Jack Monroe

THRIFTY KITCHEN

Over 120 delicious, money-saving recipes and home hacks

MORE BY JACK MONROE

A GIRL CALLED JACK

A YEAR IN 120 RECIPES

COOKING ON A BOOTSTRAP

TIN CAN COOK

VEGAN (ISH)

GOOD FOOD FOR BAD DAYS

WINNER OF . . .

THE BBC GOOD FOOD AWARD

OBSERVER FOOD MONTHLY BEST FOOD BLOG

MARIE CLAIRE WOMAN AT THE TOP

FORTNUM & MASON JUDGES' CHOICE AWARD

RED MAGAZINE INSPIRATION AWARD

OBSERVER FOOD MONTHLY PERSONALITY OF THE YEAR

WOMEN OF THE YEAR ENTREPRENEUR AWARD

WOMEN OF THE FUTURE MEDIA AWARD

EUROPEAN DIVERSITY AWARDS CAMPAIGNER OF THE YEAR

THE YMCA COURAGE AND INSPIRATION AWARD

DIVA MAGAZINE CAMPAIGNER OF THE YEAR

THE SHEILA MCKECHNIE FOUNDATION CAMPAIGNER OF THE YEAR

THRIFTY KITCHEN

'Jack Monroe's crusading work on behalf of those in food poverty would be admirable enough on its own, but she brings something very special to her activism.

She burns with a holy rage, and rightly so. Her compassion, and sometimes painful vulnerability, seem to give her the resonant strength and passionate dignity of a warrior queen.

I think it's her sensitivity that allows her to make her voice heard by those who may normally shut their ears to it without thinking twice.

Her obsessive, analytical brain means she is able to define the problems, and then come up with the solutions, succinctly. To me, she is like some sort of kitchen savant.

I can't think of another food writer with such a deep and instinctive understanding of the alchemy of cooking; she sees patterns and possibilities that can elude others. Jack is a culinary anarchist; one with a finely tuned palate and the stamina for untiring experimentation. She absolutely needs to get it right, and, she always does.'

Nigella Lawson — *The Food Programme*, BBC Radio 4

For my son, Jonathon, who has spent much of the last twelve years faithfully keeping ringpulls, picking up the postman's discarded elastic bands, pointing out bargains in the supermarket, popping another jumper on, rinsing margarine tubs, being my chief recipe tester (if he doesn't like it, it doesn't get past the draft stage), being happy with our little lot, and generally being hilarious, resilient, thoughtful, clever, generous and utterly delightful. I know I say it every time, but this could be the book that lands us our forever home. Maybe. If you tell all your friends about it, and I tell all my friends about it, well that'll shift eight whole copies. And that's a start.

Everything I do, I do it for you.

(Including mincing the mushrooms so they're undetectable in the Bolognese.)

CONTENTS

INTRODUCTION

In The Beginning

I've been writing budget cookery books for almost a decade now. It's not what I thought I would be doing with my life, ten years ago, sitting in a Fire and Rescue Service Control Room answering 999 calls, and training hard to move over to the fireground in the next round of internal recruitment, but it's where I have accidentally – and then absolutely doggedly – ended up. As I write this today, I am no longer living in the grinding, miserable poverty of my previous years, but I am still incredibly careful with how I cook, spend, shop and keep house. Partly as a way of life, partly out of fear of returning back to The Bad Times, partly because being a freelance writer is incredibly mercurial in terms of income and stability, and partly because more and more people up and down the UK and across the world are turning to thriftier lifestyles – whether by choice or through a lack of choices – and my work seems to be a little bit useful to some people. I hope that's the case here – that you may find something within these pages to help reduce your shopping bill, expand your culinary repertoire, make use of odds and sods, be a little friendlier to the planet by making single-use plastics into many-years-of-use plastics, and more. And that the tips and tricks contained within give you a little breathing room in your household budgets, a little joy in your days, and a tiny flicker of peace when you go to bed at night.

Frugality can be exhausting, complicated and overwhelming; I've tried here to make some elements of it genuinely enjoyable, simple and very gently life-changing instead. It won't make everything easier overnight, but it may make some things a little better, one day, one tin of budget tomatoes, one extra pound in your pocket, at a time.

The Here and Now

Almost a decade sits between me and my accidentally viral blog post, *Hunger Hurts*, where I documented the realities of life as a job-searching single mother in the pit of both a recession and depression, snarled up in a confusing and hostile welfare maze, clinging to my young son with an irrational fear of losing him because he was all I had in the world. I continue to talk and write about poverty because it is incredibly rare for working-class voices to break through to mainstream media platforms, and lived experiences of poverty are often shrouded in the apologetic whispers of shame, isolation, loneliness, depression, desolation and denial.

Over the last decade the queues at the food banks have grown larger, as they have been casually and deliberately ingrained into an informal support structure for the brutally decimated welfare and social care support system. Where once queuing for a food parcel in the sixth richest economy in the world would have been a stain on our national conscience, now it's such a casual part of popular culture that collection baskets are in almost every supermarket, and used as background props in television game shows. While I vehemently abhor the need for emergency food aid in this country, I also urge people to support their local food bank, as and when you can. Proselytizing about the indignity of unmet basic human needs is futile when in the immediate here and now, millions of our neighbours are going hungry behind closed doors. First we feed the people, then we plan the revolution.

So if you can, and perhaps if you find yourself saving a little on your weekly shop with this book, donate to your local food bank. Pasta, rice, ambient meals like tinned curries, noodle pots and packets, tinned meats and fish, cereals, long-life milk, period products, hearty big soups, it all helps. Every item goes directly to a person in need in your community who, without your help, may have gone hungry. And until not one single person needs the help of a food bank or other community hunger-relief organization in this country, those of us who can afford to give a little to keep their vital and often literally life-saving work going, should try to do so.

And now, here's a handful of the recipes, frugal-living tips, zero-waste food ideas and other hopefully simple ideas that have kept me and my Small Boy – who isn't so small any more – going for the last ten years. I hope you find some of it mildly inspiring, a bit useful and adaptable for your own household needs and circumstances. Every one of these recipes has been given the thumbs-up from my 12-year-old, and most of them foisted on my friends and family, and I'm genuinely excited to share every single one of them with you. Let's go.

FIRST, ASSEMBLE YOUR TOOLKIT

BASIC KITCHEN EQUIPMENT

This isn't a list of strict 'essentials' by any means – I always suggest that you start from where you are and use what you have to hand. Almost all of the recipes in this book use or are adaptable to the bare minimum of equipment; this list is an example of things that have made my life and cooking a bit easier over the years, but you definitely don't need to rush out and get everything at once. Most of these items are available cheaply from big supermarkets or high-street discount retailers, but do keep your eyes peeled in charity shops, thrift stores and boot sales as well – I get a lot of my kitchen stuff secondhand, secure in the knowledge that if a 1970s enamel floral saucepan has survived in good nick for the last fifty years, it'll probably serve me well for a wee while to come.

First things first, the key bits and pieces:

Small paring knife Big heavy chef's knife Kitchen scissors Wooden spoon Measuring jug Large sieve (doubles as a colander) Can opener Grater A large mixing bowl Some tea towels Washable dishcloths Freezer bags or other food storage Permanent marker Medium saucepan with a lid Huge non-stick pan with a lid Couple of baking sheets Couple of roasting tins of varying sizes Jars with lids in varying sizes

You might also want to add, at some point:

Serrated bread knife (useful for squashes and swedes) Knife sharpener **Chopping board, the bigger the better** Serving tongs Metal serving spoon **Loaf tin Whisk** A griddle pan **A single-egg frying pan (excellent for pancakes)** Small bullet blender, or powerful jug blender **Potato peeler** Masher Cake tin or two **Fairy cake tin** Muffin tin Casserole pot with lid **Oven gloves** Some more wooden spoons Extra knives

It would be really nice to have these extra bits, if you can wangle it:

Julienne peeler Small veg chopper or a food processor **Electric whisk** Digital scales Several food-safe spray bottles **Baking parchment** Slow cooker Spatula/fish slice **Someone nice to do the washing up, occasionally**

IF YOU DON'T HAVE THIS, TRY THIS

ROLLING PIN An empty glass bottle, or full soft drinks can, will do a pretty good job in the absence of a rolling pin. For pastry, fill a glass bottle five-sixths full – around 625ml – with cold water and shove the cork back in firmly. Freeze it until solid. The combination of cool glass and ice-cold centre will keep your pastry beautifully cold and easy to work with. Plastic juice bottles tend to have ridges in them, which isn't ideal, but they work better than having nothing to hand at all.

MASHER A combination of a solid fork and a wooden spoon will do the trick, with a bit of oomph behind it. Mash with the tines (prongs) of the fork, then beat vigorously with the wooden spoon. Repeat until it's your desired consistency. I like to do this while watching the news – I find the general underpinning rage is an excellent driving force for smashing potatoes to a pulp.

FOOD-SAFE SPRAY BOTTLES Empty Frylight bottles or similar, cleaned thoroughly and with the labels peeled off, make for lovely neat bottles to refill with your own homemade frying spray, dressings, marinades, vinegars, or whatever you fancy. Clean out the nozzle with very hot water and spray until it's all released.

WASHABLE DISHCLOTHS Cut up old pillowcases/shirts, and trim the edges as and when they start to fray. You can sew the edges if you have a needle and thread and that particular skill, or you can fold them flat and iron them, then glue them down. Wait for the glue to dry completely, then fold again, iron underneath a tea towel so the glue doesn't stick to the iron plate, and repeat to finish it neatly. The glue won't hold forever, but it will do an alright job at a pinch.

COLANDER A large sieve will do the same job as a colander, but if you don't have one of those either, hold your large chef's knife flat against the lip of the pan, leaving just millimetres for the water to escape, but not the food! Pour over the sink, holding tightly and shaking gently, until well drained.

You can also strain small amounts of non-messy foods, like pasta and rice, through a large clean square of cotton. Pop the cotton square loosely into a large bowl, making sure all four corners are hanging generously over the side. Pour your pasta or rice into the middle of the square, then quickly, before the hot water has a chance to seep into those corners, gather all four up and hold over the bowl until the water drains away. You can do a more complicated version of this with a specific cloth, four small key rings or miniature carabinas, and a large S hook slung around the tap, but it's probably easier to get a colander than all of those. But if you happen to be stuck in a preppers bunker in the apocalypse with a load of industrial survivalist camping gear, it might be helpful to know how to drain pasta.

TEA TOWELS Cotton T-shirts are super absorbent, so cut any old, stained, ill-fitting or charity shop finds into cloths around 25cm square. Again, you can hem them or glue the edges down to prevent fraying, but I just trim them if they start to look a little scrappy. It's a rag for drying dishes with, not an entry for London Fashion Week.

A LID FOR YOUR PAN A larger sturdy dinner plate, bigger pan, or a baking sheet or tray slung on top will all contain the heat instead.

EGG RINGS Tuna tin or similar squat/ short tin, both ends taken off carefully with a can opener, sanded smooth with a piece of sandpaper, and washed well after sanding to remove any tiny dusty bits of metal.

JARS Save the jars from jams, sauces, pickles etc. Soak them in soapy water to loosen the label, then scrub off any bits or glue that stubbornly remain. I number my jars on the bottom with a permanent marker, and lids on the top, so it's easy to see which one matches which and avoid ill-fitting lids, which can cause food to spoil.

LOST JAR LIDS Cut a square of paper 1cm bigger than the mouth of the jar, and secure with an elastic band or string tied tightly around it.

FREEZER BAG CLIPS Small metal bulldog clips from a stationery shop are far cheaper, stronger, and much more durable than plastic clips. You can also secure open bags by folding the corners in, tightly rolling the top down as far as it will go, and securing with a small piece of sellotape. Doing this with cereal makes it last longer by expelling the excess air that makes it go stale, so it's worth taking a few seconds to do it!

TIN CAN OPENER You'll need a small sharp knife that you're not particularly attached to, a hammer or mallet, a bit of vigour, some patience and a VERY steady hand.

FOOD STORAGE CONTAINERS
Margarine containers are a great size for storing all kinds of meals, so when you're finished with them, give them a new lease of life!

KITCHEN ROLL Newspaper works just fine for mopping up spills, cleaning windows, lining drawers or fridge shelves, etc. Rub it between your finger and thumb to make sure the ink isn't smeary – and if your digits come away clean, it'll do a great job.

STORE-CUPBOARD GOODIES

This list may look a little daunting at first glance, but you certainly don't need to rush out and buy it all at once. Pop a few items from each category on your weekly shop, or as you're able to, and in time you will build up a versatile store cupboard of basics that will form the bedrocks of literally hundreds of different meals. At the time of writing this book, the options given below were the cheapest across the major supermarkets, but they do shake their ranges up every now and again, so keep your eyes peeled for better bargains. And if you happen to find any really spectacular savings, don't keep them to yourself! Ping me a tweet (twitter.com/BootstrapCook) or tag me on Instagram (instagram.com/jack_monroe) so I can share the good news around!

Protein:

Tinned sardines or pilchards Tinned anchovies (so much flavour for their tiny size and very reasonably priced) Crab paste or salmon paste, or both Frozen white fish fillets Frozen chicken breasts or chunks Frozen sausages Chicken wings Dried red lentils Dried yellow split peas Dried green lentils Tinned kidney beans Dried or tinned chickpeas Dried or tinned cannellini or other white beans Eggs Long-life UHT milk Milk powder

Carbs:

Dried pasta Dried spaghetti Rice Oats Plain flour Tinned potatoes

Fruit:

Frozen berries Tinned pineapple
Tinned mandarins Tinned peaches Tinned pears
Tinned prunes Dried sultanas

Vegetables:

Tinned tomatoes ('peeled plum' contain more
tomatoes than 'chopped') Tinned carrots Tinned
sweetcorn Frozen spinach Frozen green beans
Frozen peas Frozen broccoli Frozen peppers
Frozen cauliflower

Flavours and Basics:

Sunflower or vegetable oil Salt Black pepper Garlic
Mustard Vinegar Bottled lemon juice Coconut milk
Mixed dried herbs Stock cubes (chicken or vegetable
are all-rounders) Paprika (sweet is versatile, smoked
gives you bang for your buck) Chilli flakes or powder
Curry powder Cumin (seeds or ground) Bicarb of
soda Stuffing mix Gravy granules Tomato ketchup
Tea bags Dark chocolate Sugar

PEOPLE ALWAYS ASK ME:

WHAT'S MY SECRET WEAPON FOR KEEPING MY WEEKLY FOOD SHOP TO UNDER £20 FOR 2 ADULTS AND 1 VERY ACTIVE AND PERPETUALLY HOLLOW PRE-TEEN?

READ ON TO FIND OUT MY SIMPLE SYSTEM, OTHERWISE KNOWN AS

'THE QUARTERHACK' . . .

THE QUARTERHACK

Before I write my shopping list, I write a whole other pre-shopping list first. Now, this may seem daunting and like a lot of work the first time you do it, but it gets quicker and easier every time as you familiarize yourself with the system, and what you have in and where it's generally kept. Taking these few moments could possibly save you hundreds of pounds a year – or even a month, depending where your budget is at the moment – on your food shopping, so give it a go and see what happens.

I try to do this Quarterhack (that my friends teasingly call my Stocktake Syndrome) every other week – which is frequently enough to keep on top of what I have in, but not so often that I resent it. You may want to do it more often, or less often, or even just every now and again. Let me explain how it works.

The Method

First, I get an A4 sheet of paper, and divide it into four vertical columns. (Hence the name, the 'quarterhack'!) Then I label each one: Protein, Carbohydrate, Fruit and Veg, and Snacks.

Then, with this in hand, I go through the fridge, freezer and kitchen cupboards, and note down every single thing that I have in stock. (Every now and then when I'm feeling extra meticulous I weigh it all, but that's a lot of work, so usually I just estimate how many portions there are by sight.)

Using a highlighter pen, I highlight the items that need using up pretty much immediately. Fresh produce nearing its use-by date, meats or other items that have been open for a couple of days in the fridge, any fruit or veg on the turn or beyond, and, using bits from the other columns, I start to plan meals around them to have over the next couple of days.

I plan a meal by starting with the protein first, because I found that cooking on a really tight budget, my instinct was to fill up with cheap starchy carbs, because they're cheap, and they make you feel full pretty much immediately. But that full feeling doesn't last, and we can't live on white rice and pasta alone, as delicious as they are. I still have these things, a LOT, but by starting with the protein element of a meal I'm nourishing my body, giving it a satisfied fullness that lasts a few hours rather than a quick-fix bloat that disappears as quickly as it comes on, and contributing to healthy muscle repair, hair and nails, and a balanced diet. I then work across the columns, picking a protein, a carb, and a fruit or veg or sometimes both, to help create balanced and varied meals.

This method quickly starts to identify where the 'gaps' are – perhaps there are a lot of proteins kicking around, like beans, canned or frozen fish, pulses, bacon, but not much fruit or veg? Or maybe a surfeit of frozen veg, but no fresh fruit? I take a second piece of paper, and make the four columns again – this is to be my Shopping List.

This is the important bit: the purpose of the Shopping List is to fill the gaps in the Stocktake List, so use the Stocktake List as a guide and plan to use as much of what you have in already as possible for the upcoming week's meals. If you're running low on fruit or veg, pick up some of that – and remember, frozen and tinned all count! If you're completely out of whole grains, grab some fortified cereal, brown rice, or similar.

It does mean being a bit organized, and because I've tried to explain it clearly, it probably seems like a lot of work, but really it's just a lot of words on my part to try to be as helpful as possible! I talked about this on Twitter a while ago and hundreds of people got in touch afterwards to say that they had done it, and that they had saved an absolute fortune on their food shop, been more creative in the kitchen, eaten better, and really enjoyed the sense of control it gave them in increasingly uncertain times.

I'm aware that this probably comes across as a bit mad, but having lived with completely empty store cupboards and relying on a weekly food bank parcel to feed myself and my son, I can have a tendency to hoard food because of the deep-rooted fear of ever being in that situation again. I know I'm not alone in this, either. Doing a regular stocktake helps to reassure me that I'm doing okay, and also keeps my hoarding tendencies in check: when you're counting every tin on a regular basis, you suddenly lose the enthusiasm for stockpiling twelve of everything!

It's a system I've tweaked and honed over the years, and there may be elements of it that don't work for you, and that's fine. There's no one-size-fits-all solution to this stuff. But I find that it refreshes the way that I cook by forcing me to put ingredients together that I may not have considered and finding ways to make them work. It's reduced a lot of my anxiety around food, has definitely reduced me impulse purchasing things that I don't need, reduces food waste because you're constantly rotating through what needs using at any given time, and keeps the food bill super low without feeling like a compromise.

I am painfully aware that 'check what you have in' is very limited in its usefulness when all you have in your cupboard is stale air and depression. I've been there, and it sucks, and I'm sorry. And furious that anyone should still be in the situation I was in in 2012/13, ten years later.

A sheet of A4 paper folded into four isn't going to solve the food poverty crisis overnight, but it may help some people feel a bit less rubbish about their budget and circumstances, and that's something, at least.

BREADS AND BREAKFAST

Look, I'll level with you here. Breakfast in our household is, nine times out of ten, a bowl of cheap honey nut cornflakes with a splash of milk, or porridge with an unfashionable amount of sugar, eaten standing up beside the kettle, waiting impatiently for my first strong, black, instant coffee of the day. Sometimes we push the boat out and have toast, sometimes in a grab for some restoration of health I'll hoof a banana and an easy peeler clementine or satsuma on the side. But on occasion, it's nice to start the day with a treat or a luxurious breakfast and a catch-up over the dining table, and that's where these recipes come in.

Think of them as being for Sundays and Somedays, rather than an everyday occurrence. I literally cook for a living, and even I don't want to start every single morning with a mountain of washing up! It's absolutely okay to have cereal most of the time. It's what it was invented for.

COURGETTE AND CHEESE SODA BREAD ⓥ

Delicious when eaten soft and warm from the oven, toasted with marmalade spread thickly on top, as a chunky homage to a grilled cheese, or doused in a beaten egg and gently fried for an irreverently Irish twist on French toast.

MAKES 1 DECENT-SIZED LOAF

oil, for greasing

250ml milk

2 tbsp lemon juice, fresh or bottled

400g self-raising flour

1½ level tsp bicarbonate of soda

1 large courgette or 2 small ones, finely or thickly grated according to preference

50g strong cheese: mature Cheddar, feta or Greek-style salad cheese, blue cheese all work here

Preheat the oven to 160°C/fan 140°C/325°F/gas 3 and make sure there is a shelf at or just below the centre of it. Lightly grease a 450g loaf tin and set to one side.

Measure the milk into a jug or mug and add the lemon juice, squeezing in the juice from a lemon half or measuring in the bottled stuff. Stir to combine and stand it to one side for about 10 minutes to curdle. It will look grim, but it's doing science, so give it the respect it deserves.

Meanwhile, weigh the flour into a large mixing bowl and add the bicarbonate of soda. Mix through thoroughly. Fold the courgette and the cheese through to distribute evenly, but do not overmix, as the moisture can start to form little clumps of dough, and we don't want that just yet.

Pour the curdled milk and lemon juice into the centre of the bowl and mix well to form a very sticky dough. This doesn't need kneading, so if it's a little goopy, that's absolutely ideal.

Tip the dough into your prepared loaf tin and shake gently to distribute it into the corners. Don't worry about smoothing the top – soda bread is meant to be delightfully knobbly! Pop it into the oven on the middle shelf and bake for 1 hour, or until a knife inserted in the centre comes out completely clean.

Remove the tin from the oven and allow to cool for 30 minutes, before turning out the loaf onto a wire rack to cool completely. You can leave it in the tin if you don't have a wire rack, but bear in mind that this retains some of the moisture from residual steam, and the bread will be a little softer and heavier for it. Not a bad thing, by any means.

Slice and serve warm or allow to cool completely and wrap in cling film or tin foil to keep fresh.

TO KEEP: Keep tightly wrapped or in an airtight container for 2–3 days, or slice and freeze for up to 4 months.

PRUNE AND PUMPKIN SEED TOAST (Ve)

A nifty use for a tin of prunes, this bread is subtly sweet enough to still be a great pairing for cheese on toast, peanut butter, or just plain hot with butter or your fave substitute spread. If you really can't abide the idea of prunes, replace them with tinned pears instead. I used pumpkin seeds because it's what I happened to have in at the time (I get them cheap from my local greengrocer), but you can use any kind of seeds or nuts in their place. Sunflower seeds work well, as do mixed chopped nuts.

MAKES 1 LARGE LOAF, AROUND 14 SLICES

1 x 400g tin of prunes, including juice

500g plain flour, plus extra for dusting

a few pinches of salt

100g pumpkin or other seeds

10g dried active yeast

oil, for greasing

First, drain the prunes, reserving the juice, and de-stone them. This is fairly easily done by pinching one between finger and thumb and giving it a squeeze – the stone should just slither out. Pop the stones in your compost bin or food waste, and set the prunes to one side in a bowl. Pour the juice into a measuring jug and set to one side.

Weigh the flour into your mixing bowl and add a few generous pinches of salt, the seeds and the yeast. Stir it all together to evenly distribute.

Add warm water to your reserved prune juice to make the liquid up to 400ml in total – it shouldn't be too hot otherwise you will kill off the yeast – and you're relying on that to make your bread rise, so don't scald it! Add the prunes to the liquid, and pour into your dry ingredients.

Mix well with either a well-oiled blunt knife or a rubber spatula, to bring the dough together. If it's crumbly, add a splash more water. If it's slightly sticky, add a tablespoon of flour.

When the dough is well combined, tip it onto a floured work surface, and knead for around 7–8 minutes. I prefer to oil my hands rather than flour them; it incorporates fat into the loaf which helps with the overall crumb structure, and prevents it from sticking to either the worktop or your hands.

When the dough is springy and the prunes are pretty much pulverized, pop it into a well-oiled bowl (I use the mixing bowl that I made the dough in in the first place to pick up any stray bits that are clinging to the sides) and cover. I pop a clean Bag For Life over the top of mine and place it in the warmest part of the house for 2–3 hours, until doubled in size. How long it takes to rise will depend on the temperature and humidity of your home – if it's really struggling to get going, you can pop it in the microwave on the defrost setting for a few minutes to give it a head start.

When risen, lightly grease a 900g (fairly standard sized) loaf tin and transfer your dough to it, shaking gently from side to side so it roughly takes on the shape of the tin. Re-cover with your bag or wrap and leave for another 30–45 minutes to prove – this is known as the 'proving stage' in bread baking, and it helps you to produce a lovely light loaf.

Preheat the oven to 200°C/fan 180°C/400°F/gas 6 and place a roasting dish or ovenproof bowl in the bottom. Add an inch or two of water, and close the door for 10 minutes. This helps to generate steam in your oven, keeping your loaf moist and preventing a too-hard crust from forming.

When the oven is good and steamy, turn it down to 160°C/fan 140°C/325°F/gas 3, and place the loaf tin in the centre.

Bake for 1 hour, until risen and golden, then allow to cool for 20 minutes in the tin before turning out to finish cooling.

TO KEEP: It will keep for 4 days in an airtight bag or container – I find the inner baggies from cereal boxes make excellent bread bags, and they're almost endlessly reusable, too.

OATY SODA BREAD Ⓥ

This is an ideal starter recipe for those who haven't made bread before or who have had a disastrous experience with it in the past. There's barely any kneading, no strict water temperatures to think about, no rising and proving time, just a quick fling together of some very basic ingredients and bung it in the oven. If you think making bread is difficult or intimidating, start here. You'll surprise yourself.

MAKES 1 DECENT-SIZED LOAF

oil, for greasing

1 tbsp light-coloured vinegar or lemon juice, fresh or bottled

400ml milk

500g plain flour, plus extra for dusting

½ tsp salt

75g porridge oats, plus extra for sprinkling

2 tsp bicarbonate of soda

Preheat the oven to 180°C/fan 160°C/350°F/gas 4 and make sure there is a shelf at or just below the centre of it. Lightly grease a 450g loaf tin and set to one side.

In a measuring jug, measure the vinegar or lemon juice into the milk. Set the jug to one side for about 5 minutes to allow the liquid to curdle and separate.

Meanwhile, weigh the flour, salt and oats into a bowl, add the bicarbonate of soda and mix through.

Make a well (a kind of shallow hole) in the centre of the flour and pour in most of the milk–acid mixture. Mix well with a wooden spoon to form a sticky dough.

Tip the dough onto a floured work surface and pat into a round shape, kneading it ever so lightly but briefly, as there's no yeast to activate here, so you just need to smooth the dough and shape it rather than give it the standard 10-minute pummelling treatment.

Pop the shaped dough into the loaf tin, score a line on top of the dough down the middle about 1cm deep with a sharp knife, dust with a little extra flour and scatter some oats on top.

Bake in the oven for 40 minutes. Once cooked through, the loaf should sound hollow on the bottom when tipped out and tapped, and feel ridiculously light.

Remove the tin from the oven, turn out the soda bread whilst hot and leave to cool on a wire rack. Break into chunks and serve warm with butter.

TO KEEP: Allow to cool completely, then wrap in cling film or place in an airtight food storage bag, squeezing as much air out as possible, to keep fresh. Will keep for up to 3 days – soda bread does tend to harden quite quickly, but if this happens, it makes an excellent fried slice with an egg on top!

GET UP AND GO MUFFINS ⓥ

You can use the entire banana – skin and all – in these muffins if you have a blender or a food processor (mine is an old Moulinex that was £12 from a local charity shop, easily as old as I am and still going strong!). If you don't have a blender you can slice the skin very finely – like matchstick-fine – and still smuggle it in. The muffins can be easily made vegan or dairy free by using a plant-based milk of your choice, too.

MAKES 12 MUFFINS

75ml light cooking oil, plus extra for greasing

125ml milk

1 tsp bottled lemon juice

1 x 400g tin of prunes in juice

2 large ripe bananas or 3 tiddlers

75g porridge oats

175g self-raising flour

1½ tsp baking powder

100g sugar – any kind

Preheat the oven to 190°C/fan 170°C/375°F/gas 5, and lightly grease a 12-hole muffin tin. Pop muffin cases in each hole, if using them (sometimes I don't bother and just let them run wild in there, so if you don't have muffin cases, don't worry!).

Measure out your milk into a jug and add the lemon juice, then leave to stand to one side for a moment. The lemon juice will slightly curdle the milk; don't worry, that's exactly the result we are after!

Drain the prunes over a bowl, reserving the juice to use later. Remove the stones and discard them, then place the prunes in your blender or in a large mixing bowl.

Slice your bananas and add them to the mixing bowl or to the blender, depending on which you are using. Add the oil and mash well with a fork, or pulse in the blender until smooth. If using the blender, pour it into a mixing bowl.

However you achieve your prune-banana mixture, once it's in the mixing bowl and well combined, add the oats, flour, baking powder and sugar, and mix well to combine. Pour in the milk and lemon juice mixture, and continue to mix to form a thick batter. Add a splash of the reserved prune juice to loosen it, and then another, until you have the consistency of a fairly thick cake batter.

Bake in the centre of the oven for 22–25 minutes, until risen and a small sharp knife inserted into the centre of one comes out clean.

TO KEEP: These will keep in an airtight container, tin or food-safe bag for up to 4 days, or in the freezer for 6 months.

BANANA PEEL PANCAKES ⓥ

An ideal use for past-their-best bananas, these pancakes are delicious on their own, drenched in syrup, with a little chocolate, or topped with frozen, fresh or tinned fruit. I've tested this recipe over the years with various plant-based milks and can confirm it works well with oat, soya, coconut, almond, cashew, hazelnut, hemp and rice milk, if dairy milk isn't your kind of thing. It also works with tinned coconut milk and UHT milk if you find yourself in need of pancakes in a post-apocalyptic wasteland. I guess I like to prepare snacks for all eventualities.

SERVES 2–4

2 bananas, including peel
2 tbsp oil
100ml milk or plant-
   based equivalent
100g self-raising flour

Finely slice your bananas and pop them into a mixing bowl, along with 1 tablespoon of the oil and your milk. Mash with a fork or masher to a smooth pulp, beating well with the tines (prongs) of the fork to knock out any lumps. Very finely slice the banana peel and add that too. If you have a small bullet blender, mini chopper or food processor you may wish to put the banana flesh and peel in and whizz it up to smooth, if the idea of eating banana peel is one you need to smuggle past your household, for example!

Add your flour and beat well to combine to a thick smooth batter.

Heat the remaining oil in a frying pan and dollop the batter in 2 tablespoons at a time. Fry for a few minutes on each side until golden and crisp at the edges, carefully turning over halfway through. Repeat until all of the batter is used, then serve immediately.

TO KEEP: Leftovers will keep, covered, in the fridge for 2 days, or the freezer for 3 months. Warm through completely to serve.

FRENCH TOAST ⓥ

French toast, also known as 'eggy bread', is one of my son's favourite timeless breakfasts, and has been since he was very small. You can serve it savoury, with beans or tinned plum tomatoes on top, or sweet with warm berries, a dollop of jam or marmalade pinged in the microwave to melt it into a coulis-style sauce, or my favourite of all, lemon curd.

SERVES 2

2 eggs
120ml milk
a few pinches of
    ground cinnamon
4 slices of bread
2 tbsp light cooking oil
grilled banana or warmed
    frozen berries, to serve

Carefully crack your eggs into a wide, shallow bowl. Add the milk and cinnamon, and beat well until well combined and evenly coloured.

Place the bread into the dish, turning over after a minute or two to allow both sides to soak up the milky eggy mixture.

Heat the oil in a frying pan or griddle pan, then turn down to a medium heat to stop it from smoking excessively. Place the bread in, as many slices as will comfortably fit – you may need to do it in batches. Fry for 3 minutes on each side, until crisp at the edges and golden in colour, then remove and continue with the remaining slices until all are cooked through.

Serve immediately while hot, with your topping of choice.

RASPBERRY AND LEMON CURD BAKED OATS ⓥ

You can use any fresh or frozen berries in this simple baked oats recipe – or even dollops of jam or applesauce at a pinch! The lemon curd is a lovely touch, but marmalade works as a substitute if you don't have any in. Failing that, a dash of lemon juice and a sprinkling of sugar provides the same contrasting tart sweetness in a tight spot.

SERVES 2

oil, for greasing
60g porridge oats
120g natural yoghurt
120g raspberries or other berries
2–4 tbsp lemon curd, to taste

Preheat the oven to 160°C/fan 140°C/325°F/gas 3 and make sure there is a shelf roughly in the centre of it. Lightly grease a 20cm cake tin or roasting tin.

Weigh your porridge oats into your tin – there's no point messing up a mixing bowl here and creating more washing up! Add your yoghurt, then your berries, and stir well to combine.

Dollop the lemon curd on top, and spread with the back of a spoon to lightly coat the top layer, then place in the oven.

Bake for 40 minutes, until the oats are swollen and slightly golden at the edges.

Remove carefully from the oven and serve immediately. You can enjoy these as they are, or add a splash or milk or natural yoghurt if you like.

TO KEEP: Leftovers can be chilled in the fridge and enjoyed warm or cold over the next 3 days.

WARM SUNSHINE OATS (Ve)

These baked oats taste like a tropical dessert – somewhere between a flapjack and a crumble, but for breakfast! A quick and simple way to get some fruit into the family; and entirely made from store-cupboard ingredients. You can use fruit in juice or in syrup for this recipe; the latter will be sweeter, the former will have a stronger citrus flavour. *(Pictured on previous page)*

SERVES 4

1 small tin of mandarins, around 300g

1 large tin of pineapple chunks, around 540g

75g mixed dried fruit or sultanas

120g porridge oats

a pinch of cinnamon (optional)

Preheat the oven to 180°C/fan 160°C/350°F/gas 4, and make sure there is a shelf roughly in the centre of it.

Using a sieve and a measuring jug, strain the liquid well from both tins into the jug – I press my fruit gently into the sieve to get the most out of it without squishing it to a pulp. Check how much there is; if the liquid is short of 350ml, make up the difference by adding cold tap water.

Pour the drained and the dried fruit and oats into a 20cm ovenproof dish, and stir gently to fold the fruit through and evenly distribute it. Pour over the strained liquid and stir again. Top with the cinnamon, if using.

Bake in the centre of the oven for 40 minutes, until plump and golden. Remove from the oven and allow to cool for a few minutes before serving. The oats can be enjoyed as they are, or with a splash of milk or dollop of yoghurt, if you like.

TO KEEP: Cool completely and store, covered, in the fridge for up to 3 days. Enjoy cold with yoghurt, or warmed through with a splash of milk.

LEMON AND BERRY DUTCH BABIES Ⓥ

'Dutch babies' are an adorably named cross between a sweet Yorkshire pudding and a large pancake, dropped into a pan and cooked on the hob or in the oven and filled with whatever you fancy. I have made a fruit cocktail and custard version in the past, which was delicious, but this deceptively decadent version is my favourite. If you don't have lemon curd in the house, any marmalade or red jam will do – simply ping it in the microwave for a few seconds to loosen it before dolloping it on.

MAKES 4

2 medium eggs

2 tbsp caster sugar, plus extra for serving

150ml any kind of milk

100g plain flour

100g berries – fresh or frozen or canned, any will do

3 tbsp lemon curd or marmalade

4 tsp light cooking oil or margarine or butter

TIP: *I like to use either Yorkshire pudding trays or a muffin tin for this recipe, but you could also use a 20cm round cake tin or thereabouts, or a 20cm ovenproof non-stick shallow pan.*

First make your batter – on lazy days or sore-joints days I simply fling the eggs, sugar, milk, and flour into my small bullet blender and whizz it to a super-smooth consistency, but you can crack the eggs into a bowl, beat them together with the sugar and slowly add the milk and flour instead for the same end result.

Pop your batter in the fridge to chill out for a while – around 30 minutes is fine. While the batter chills out, make the lemon–berry filling. Pop the berries into a microwave-safe mug, and ping on a high heat for 1 minute for fresh ones, or 2 minutes for frozen. Spoon the lemon curd over the top, and stir in to melt in the residual heat of the piping-hot and juicy berries. Leave to firm up a little on the side while the batter chills.

When your batter is chilled, preheat the oven to 200°C/fan 180°C/400°F/ gas 6 and ensure there is a shelf set in the centre. Divide the oil evenly between your Yorkshire pudding trays, if using them, or pour it into the cake tin. Place the tin – not the batter, not yet – into the oven for 5–6 minutes to get it super hot. Remove it carefully. Pour in the batter and immediately return it to the oven for 14 minutes. Do not be tempted to open the door until those 14 minutes are up!

When ready, carefully remove the buns from the tin (or tray) and top with the lemon and berry mixture. Serve immediately, dredged with extra sugar if you really can't help yourself.

TO KEEP: Cool and cover, and pop in the fridge for up to 2 days. Warm through to serve.

MONSTER BUMS (Ve)

These bright green little wonders are a sneaky way of smuggling veg and vitamins into my young son, and they make for a good conversation starter! Use them as burger buns, for sandwiches, or dunking into soup – the spinach flavour is almost undetectable, but the colour is a delight. And 'bums' here isn't a spelling error, it's a puerile hark back to the first time I made these for my son when he was much younger, and squished two little round buns together before baking them to make him laugh. The things we do to get some green things into our children sometimes . . .

MAKES 8 BUNS

2 generous fistfuls of fresh spinach or defrosted frozen spinach

1 generous fistful of parsley

400ml warm water

500g plain flour, plus extra for dusting

2 tsp (10g) dried active yeast

1 tbsp cooking oil

a pinch of salt

First pop the greens and parsley into a blender, along with the water, and blitz until liquidized. Pop a sieve or fine-mesh strainer over a mixing bowl, and strain to catch any large remaining pieces. Add the flour, yeast, oil and salt, and mix to form a dough. I use the blunt side of a butter knife to mix dough, pushing it around the bowl all the way to the edges to catch any stray streaks of flour.

Generously flour your worktop, then tip the dough onto it. Knead for 5–10 minutes until springy, then return it to the mixing bowl. Cover and leave in a warm place for 3 hours to rise.

When risen, the dough should have at least doubled in size. Tip it back onto a floured worktop and divide into eight pieces. Lightly grease or flour a flat baking tray. Roll the eight pieces gently into squat little balls and place on the baking tray, a couple of inches apart. Leave for a further hour to prove.

Preheat the oven to 160°C/fan 140°C/325°F/gas 3 and make sure there is a shelf roughly in the centre of it.

Bake the buns in the centre of the oven for 50 minutes, or until risen. They might be slightly golden on the outside, but they should be bright green in the middle. Enjoy!

TO KEEP: Allow to cool completely, then either wrap in cling film or pop into a food storage bag, squeezing out as much air as possible before sealing. Best enjoyed up to 3 days after making them, or they can be frozen for up to 3 months. Defrost completely at room temperature before serving.

SECRET SCRAMBLED EGGS ⓥ

These scrambled eggs are deliciously creamy and rich, without the use of any butter at all. They have won me many compliments from friends and family over the years, and now I don't do them any other way. The mayonnaise has the benefit of keeping the eggs in a suspended state of perfection for slightly longer than traditionally scrambled eggs; ideal if your household is one where you have to announce that breakfast is ready several times in escalating decibels before anybody deigns to appear to devour it.

SERVES 2

2 tbsp light cooking oil
5 medium eggs
a pinch of salt
plenty of black pepper
3 tbsp mayonnaise

Add the oil to a large, non-stick pan and crack in the eggs. Place on the smallest hob ring on the lowest heat and season generously with salt and pepper.

Cook very gently, for around 5–6 minutes, stirring almost constantly to stop them ending up overdone.

When they have almost cooked, add the mayonnaise, and stir through for another minute. Serve immediately, with more salt and pepper to taste.

PEAR AND BACON PORRIDGE

This is one of my son's favourite breakfasts; it feels super luxurious but it's really cheap and simple! If you can't spare the milk you can make it with all water instead, just stir it well to release the creamy starches from the oats and it'll be absolutely grand. If bacon isn't your thing, salted peanuts or other nuts make for a fine equivalent.

SERVES 2

100g porridge oats

300ml milk, or your
  fave equivalent

300ml water

½ x 415g tin of pears,
  plus the juice

50g cooking bacon
  or other bacon

1 tbsp oil or fat

1 tbsp sugar (optional)

a pinch of ground
  cinnamon (optional)

Measure the porridge oats into a small saucepan and add the milk and water. Strain your pears, reserving the juice or syrup from the tin, and pour this into the porridge pan. Place on a high heat on the smallest hob ring for a few minutes until it comes to the boil, then reduce the heat right down to a simmer for 10–12 minutes, stirring intermittently to prevent the oats catching and burning on the bottom of the pan.

Dice the pears and roughly chop your bacon, then toss both into a frying pan, along with the oil, and also the sugar and cinnamon, if using. Place on a high heat on a large hob ring to sear and caramelize, which should take 4–5 minutes.

Serve the porridge hot with the pears and bacon (or nuts!) scattered on top.

TO KEEP: Leftovers can be stored in the fridge and used within 2 days, but they will thicken a considerable amount due to the starches in the oats, so thin any leftover mixture well before refrigerating. Warm through in the microwave or on the hob and serve piping hot.

HOMEMADE MUESLI Ⓥ

I did a lot of very nerdy, mathematical research for this recipe, because I wanted to recreate the best possible muesli for the lowest possible price. This included forensically dissecting both the cheapest supermarket brand and the most expensive high-street version, then noting down what their components were and in what quantities they appeared. I then scoured the shops looking for the cheapest versions of each of the ingredients, sorting them into their essential categories: oats, nuts or seeds, and dried fruits. Once I'd identified the cheapest items from each category, I fiddled with the quantities until I had a muesli that I was happy with. And then I realized that in the year that yawns between handing in my book manuscript to my publisher and it hitting the shelves, the prices of all of these ingredients are very likely to have changed, making my endeavour almost obsolete. But no matter, at the very least this muesli recipe exists as a snapshot into what the cheapest combination of these ingredients were in the spring of 2022, and I'm rather happy with it. Should any of the components skyrocket in price by the time you hold this book in your hands, do feel free to swap it out for something cheaper! On this note, I use salted nuts from the 'snack' section of the supermarket, as they are far cheaper than those in the fruit and veg or baking aisles, and simply soak them in cold water for an hour and pat them dry thoroughly before using. They do retain a little salty background hit, but I have to say, I rather enjoy that.

MAKES 600G, OR 15 X 40G PORTIONS

60g salted peanuts
40g salted cashew nuts
325g porridge oats
100g mixed dried fruit
30g sunflower seeds
30g pumpkin seeds
20g golden linseeds or flax seeds (optional, but an excellent source of fibre!)

First soak the salted nuts in cold water for an hour or two, then drain and rinse them thoroughly. Pat them dry thoroughly with kitchen roll or a very clean, non-fluffy tea towel, and leave them to dry. If you want to speed up this process, you can toast them briefly in a hot frying pan for about 20 seconds on the heat, jiggling them so they don't burn, then tip them out to cool down.

Weigh your oats into a large mixing bowl, and add the dry nuts, mixed dried fruit and seeds. Mix everything together thoroughly so all of the ingredients are evenly distributed, then transfer to a large squeaky-clean jar or container with an airtight lid.

TO KEEP: Keep out of direct sunlight and use within 3 months.

CINNAMON CRUNCH Ⓥ

I first made this as an alternative to a popular cinnamon cereal that my son is extremely keen on, and cereal is such a simple, help-yourself option for school runs, late mornings, quick snacks and even an after-dinner filler if you find yourself with the munchies of an eating. . . The one he loves is almost £3 for a box that he demolishes in under a week (despite serving suggestions saying it should hold 12 servings – although how much of its disappearance is owed to my hand firkling around in the box absentmindedly whenever I walk past it isn't something I'm willing to subject to personal scrutiny). At any rate, I wanted to make something that was just as delicious, packed a bit more of a protein punch, and was far kinder to my grocery budget – and this recipe was a hit all round. I quadrupled the quantities two days later, and we've had a rolling jar of it on the go in the kitchen ever since. Particularly lovely with vanilla milk, or a sprinkling of dark brown sugar, too. (Pictured on previous page)

MAKES 270G, OR 9 PORTIONS

30ml light cooking oil, plus extra for greasing

200g porridge oats

1 tbsp or 6g ground cinnamon

a pinch or two of salt

60ml golden syrup or honey

Preheat the oven to 130°C/fan 110°C/265°F/gas 1 and make sure there is a shelf roughly in the centre of it. Lightly grease the largest baking tray or roasting tin you have that will fit in your oven (assuming here that you have a standard oven, not an industrial one!). Set it to one side for a moment.

Weigh your oats into a large mixing bowl, then add the cinnamon and a pinch or two of salt. Mix well to distribute the flavours evenly.

Drizzle over the golden syrup and the cooking oil, and mix well to lightly coat the oats. They will start to stick together – this is totally normal and completely fine, you can break it up again!

Dollop the mixture onto your prepared tray, and spread out to all four corners, breaking up any overly large clumps so they cook evenly. Place into the oven and bake for 18–20 minutes, removing the tray to gently jostle the oats or turn them over halfway through.

Remove from the oven and leave to cool completely before removing from the tray – depending on the season and the temperature of your kitchen, I would allow for around an hour, but be aware that it smells so delicious that other household members may be tempted to come and investigate it as it cools!

TO KEEP: It will keep in a very clean, airtight jar for around 6 months, but it doesn't tend to stick around that long, in my experience!

PEAR AND CINNAMON BUNS Ⓥ

Make a batch of these and freeze them individually or in pairs, then pop one out of the freezer the evening before a busy day ahead for a grab-and-go breakfast that will fuel you through your morning!

MAKES 12 BUNS

2 x 415g tins of pear halves in juice

1 tbsp dried active yeast

3 tbsp sugar

450g plain flour, plus extra for dusting

½ tsp salt

1 medium egg, plus 1 egg yolk

6 tbsp natural yoghurt

oil, for greasing

2 tsp ground cinnamon

1 tsp ground ginger

100g icing sugar

2 tbsp chopped nuts (optional)

First separate your tinned pear halves from the juice by placing a fine-mesh sieve over a large jug or mixing bowl and pouring them through one at a time. Pop the pear halves into a bowl and set to one side – you'll be coming back for these later.

Measure 160ml of the juice into a jug and pour the rest back over the pears in their bowl. Warm the jug of juice in the microwave for 60 seconds, or on the hob for a minute, until warm but not hot. Add the yeast and sugar and whisk briefly with a fork, then stand it to one side for a few minutes for the yeast to wake up and start bubbling.

While the yeast is activating, weigh your flour into a large mixing bowl. Add the salt and stir well for half a minute to combine.

Grab a small bowl or mug and crack in the egg, then add the yolk of the second. (You can use the spare white to glaze the buns, if you like, or keep it in the fridge for up to 3 days to add to another bake, scrambled eggs, an omelette or similar.) Add 4 tablespoons of yoghurt – you'll need the other two later, so don't add them here – and beat together. Add to the yeast mixture, and whisk briefly but briskly with a fork until well beaten and smooth.

Make a well in the middle of your flour, and pour in the liquid ingredients. Mix with a wooden spoon or silicone spatula to bring together in a smooth dough. If it's a bit sticky, add a tablespoon or two more flour and mix again.

Generously flour your work surface and tip the dough onto it. Knead for around 6 minutes, until it feels smooth and springy to touch. You can test this by lightly pressing a finger into the surface; if it slowly springs back into shape, it's ready. If not, continue to knead it for another minute or two.

Lightly oil a clean mixing bowl, and pop the dough into it. Cover it with cling film, a carrier bag, or a clean tea towel, and leave it to rise in the warmest part of your home for 2½ hours, or until doubled in size.

While the dough is rising, transfer your pears and reserved juice to a blender and blend until smooth. Pour into a saucepan and add the ground cinnamon and ginger. Simmer on a low heat on the smallest hob ring for around 20 minutes to thicken and reduce by around a third – cover the pan with a lid if it starts to spit, otherwise it may get a bit messy! Remove from the heat and allow to cool completely while the dough rises.

When the dough is risen and doubled in size, generously flour your work surface again, and tip it onto it. Lightly oil a rolling pin and roll out to a rectangle shape, approximately 40 x 20cm. Spoon the spiced pear puree onto the dough and spread evenly all over, all the way to the edges, using a palette knife, pastry brush or the back of a spoon.

Taking the shorter side, roll it up lightly and carefully, taking care not to push the filling out. A little spillage is inevitable, but try not to lose too much of it! When rolled up, carefully turn it so it is seam side down, to help to seal it and hold it together. Lightly grease a roasting dish approximately 30 x 20cm or thereabouts.

Using a serrated bread knife or very very sharp knife, cut into twelve equally sized pieces. They can get a little messy at this stage, so cut one piece, then carefully transfer it to the prepared dish, pressing it back together, if required, before cutting the next. Repeat until all of the dough is used up, then cover the dish and leave to prove for another hour.

When that's done, they should be all snug in their dish and touching at the edges now. Preheat the oven to 160°C/fan 140°C/325°F/gas 3, and place them on a shelf in or just below the middle of the oven. Bake for 1 hour, then remove and allow to cool completely in the dish – usually around 2 hours. Don't try to ice them while they're still warm, you'll end up with a melty, split mess!

When cool, sift the icing sugar into a mixing bowl and add the remaining 2 tablespoons of yoghurt. Mix well to form a thick icing, and spread over the top of the buns. Scatter the chopped nuts on top, if using, then leave to set.

TO KEEP: Enjoy within 3 days, storing them in a clean airtight container, or freeze for up to 3 months.

APPLE BIRCHER Ⓥ

A filling and healthy breakfast option that's a moment to rustle up the night before, Bircher pots are named after their Swiss inventor, Dr Maximilian Oskar Bircher-Benner. He first came up with the idea as part of a project to try to combat tuberculosis in the early 1900s, and originally intended it as a starter for a meal or an evening snack. The Apfeldiatspeise, as it was then known, was a resounding success, and one I have made many variations on over the years. For a luxurious version with extra flavour, you can use the muesli on page 46 as your base for this recipe, or as per the original concept, you can just use plain oats.

SERVES 2

1 medium apple

50g porridge oats or muesli (see page 46 for homemade)

150ml milk

75g natural yoghurt

nuts or seeds, to top (optional)

First grate your apple coarsely, including the skin, into a decent-sized mixing bowl.

Add your oats or muesli, then the milk and yoghurt, and stir everything well to combine. Divide it between two pots or jars and top with the nuts or seeds, if you have any to hand. Pop the pots in the fridge overnight, or for 4 hours, and enjoy cold.

TO KEEP: These can be made up to 2 days in advance but I wouldn't recommend leaving them any longer than that due to the fresh apple used, as it will start to go brown and not look very appetizing. The recipe is not particularly amenable to freezing due to the dairy content. It will freeze and thaw if you're determined to do so, but may split in the thawing process. If this happens, it's still fine to eat, just give it a really vigorous stir to bring it back together.

LIGHT BITES

For when you want something a bit less filling than a dinner, but a bit more than a bowl of cereal, the recipes in this chapter perfectly straddle the two. Some of these could be filed under 'brunch', some under 'lunch', and some 'snacks', but life isn't always that neat and tidy, so I've put them all together here and trust that you're all grown-up enough to decide exactly what you want to eat and when you want to eat it.

RADISHES OR OTHER CRUNCHY VEG WITH A TRIO OF DIPS

I love the humble radish. Cheap, abundant, very easy to grow your own with a satisfyingly speedy seed-to-plate turnaround, and a refreshing crunchy snack any time of day. I think they're vastly underrated in our national cuisine, and I'm on a slow-burning mission to evangelically bring them to as many of your fridges and stomachs as possible. I make this anchovy mayo very regularly to dunk them into, halved or whole, and the salty creamy dip is a perfect match for the peppery twang of a fresh radish, but the other two dips are also regulars in my snacking repertoire. The stretchy hummus is a bit of a travesty, but I'm Greek Cypriot, so I figure that I have a modicum of artistic licence to tinker with chickpeas in an emergency. And if you disagree, that's fine, but you're missing out on a treat! These dips work with any 'crudité' vegetables, like carrots cut into slices or batons, cucumber, celery, fresh peppers, cooked and cooled green beans, sugarsnap peas, mangetout, and more.

ANCHOVY MAYONNAISE

4 anchovies

1 tsp of the oil from the anchovy tin

100g any kind of mayonnaise

plenty of black pepper

Either finely chop the anchovies with a small sharp knife and transfer to a small bowl with the oil and mayo, and beat vigorously with a fork to combine them, or decant the whole lot into the small cup of a bullet blender or mini chopper and whizz for half a minute to combine. Stir through the black pepper.

TINNED TOMATO SALSA  (Ve)

1 x 400g tin chopped tomatoes

1 small onion

a handful of fresh parsley, basil or coriander (optional)

1 tsp mixed dried herbs

a pinch of chilli flakes or powder

1 tbsp light cooking oil

1 tsp light-coloured vinegar

a pinch of salt and black pepper

Drain the tinned tomatoes well through a sieve or a colander lined with clean kitchen roll. Reserve the strained juice in a clean bottle or jar in the fridge and add it to a Bolognese, tomato-based pasta sauce, soup or similar over the next 4 days so as not to waste it. Finely chop your onion as small as you can get it, and chop your fresh herbs if you're using them. Add the dried herbs, chilli, oil, vinegar, salt and pepper, and stir well to combine.

STRETCHY HUMMUS (V)

1 x 400g tin of
chickpeas, including
the juice from the tin

4–6 tbsp mayonnaise

Simply decant the chickpeas, aquafaba (tin juice), and mayo into the small cup of a bullet blender and blitz to combine. If you don't have a blender, tip the chickpeas and aquafaba into a mixing bowl and mash vigorously with a masher or fork for a few minutes, then mix in the mayonnaise until well combined.

TO KEEP: All of these dips will keep in a clean jar or foodsafe container – the small dip containers from takeaways are ideal for this – for up to 5 days, but it never quite lasts that long in my house!

MARMITE CRUMPETS ⓥ

Patience is most definitely a virtue with this recipe, but these are absolute heaven, and very moreish! Have them hot with butter and melted cheese – or your fave equivalent toppings. If you don't have an egg-poaching ring handy, you can just drop them onto a hot non-stick pan, or use a shallow tin, cleaned, with the top and bottom taken off with a tin opener, well stripped of the label (so it doesn't catch light!) and lightly greased. A tuna tin or a small baked bean or sweetcorn one is ideal – depending on the size you may end up with miniature crumpets, so keep an eye on what's going on in your pan and adjust the cooking time accordingly. It seems like a lot of yeast, but I've tested this a dozen times and I promise you it's absolutely right – it's where the holes come from!

MAKES 8, TO SERVE 4

2 tbsp Marmite
200ml boiling water
300ml milk (whole or unsweetened soya)
300g plain flour
2 level tbsp dried active yeast
1 tsp bicarbonate of soda
oil, for greasing

First, pop your kettle on to boil. While you're waiting, spoon the Marmite into a mug. Don't worry if it doesn't all come off the spoon, that's what the boiling water is for! Pour 200ml boiling water over the Marmite, including over the spoon to loosen the stubborn bits. Mix well until the Marmite has dissolved.

Measure your milk into a jug, then add a splash of the hot water and Marmite mixture. Just a splash right now, as you want to bring the milk to temperature gradually, not give it a shock so it curdles. It's worth a little care and patience at this stage to save you having to start over!

Add a splash more of the hot liquid, stirring it into the milk, and repeat until combined. I cannot emphasize enough how important it is to add the boiling liquid very slowly to the cold milk, especially when using soya milk! When the liquid is all combined, set it to one side for a moment.

Grab a large mixing bowl and weigh in your flour, then measure in the yeast and bicarbonate of soda. If you only have baking powder to hand, use double the amount. If you have self-raising flour instead of plain, it'll be fine. A bit fluffier than a standard crumpet perhaps, but better than no crumpets at all. Mix the dry ingredients together thoroughly to evenly distribute them. You don't need to add salt here, as the Marmite gives out quite enough of that deep savoury flavour to not need it. If you absolutely feel you need to, out of habit, just cut back on the Marmite a bit and add a pinch.

Make a well – like a kind of hole that you'd dig at the beach as a kid – in the centre of the dry ingredients. Pour in the warm liquid and stir briskly and thoroughly to form a loose, runny batter. Cover with a tea towel, old but clean T-shirt, cling film or loosely tied plastic bag, and leave somewhere warm for an hour. If it's a British winter and you don't have anywhere particularly warm, you can get it started by balancing the bowl on top of a saucepan with a couple of inches of water in and bringing it to the boil. This will kickstart the yeast, but make sure the water doesn't touch the bottom of the bowl as very

high temperatures can kill it off; it's a sensitive soul! Then cover it and stash it somewhere for at least 2 hours to give it a chance to rise.

Gently heat a frying pan on the smallest hob ring and place your poaching rings (or clean greased tin-can rings) into it. Depending on how many rings you have, you may need to do this in batches. Add a teaspoon of oil to the centre of each ring, then turn the heat down to its lowest possible setting.

When the pan is hot – which is a slow process but don't be tempted to rush it! – dollop 3 tablespoons of the batter into each ring and leave well alone for at least 10 minutes. The slow and gentle heat gives them their height and also allows the huge bubbles to develop that give crumpets their uniquely incredible texture. You'll know they're almost done when there are large bubbles forming on the top. I admit sometimes I poke mine with a chopstick to make the bubbles more defined!

When the batter on top is no longer runny, carefully run a knife around the inside of the ring and remove it. Flip the crumpet over and cook on the other side for a minute or two to seal it, then serve hot.

TO KEEP: Cool completely and store in an airtight food storage bag or tightly wrapped cling film for up to 3 days, or pop them in the freezer for up to 3 months.

ROASTED ROOTS SOUP

This sweet and spicy soup is an ideal way to use up leftover roasted or boiled vegetables – any combination of potatoes, sweet potatoes, parsnips, beetroot, carrots and onions will work. Using the liquid from a tin of chickpeas may seem odd but it gives it a silky-smooth texture. You can use cannellini beans in place of chickpeas, if you like.

SERVES 4

1 large onion

300g mixed roasted root vegetables

2 tbsp light cooking oil

1 x 400g tin of chickpeas, including the liquid

1 tbsp medium curry powder

½ tsp English mustard

1 chicken or vegetable stock cube

a pinch of salt

plenty of black pepper

bread or blue cheese (optional)

Peel and slice your onion, and roughly chop the root vegetables. Heat the oil in a large non-stick pan and fry the veg for 4–5 minutes. Transfer to a blender along with the chickpeas and all of the liquid from the tin. Add your curry powder, mustard, stock cube and enough cold water to just about cover everything. Blend to a thick smooth consistency and transfer back to the pan. Thin with additional water until it is your desired consistency, and season to taste with salt and pepper.

You can tear up and fry leftover bread to top this with crunchy croutons, or drop in diced pieces of cheese to melt on the top. I like a soft blue cheese myself – which sounds like an odd combination but the pungent flavour and creamy smoothness really work well with this sweet and spicy soup.

TO KEEP: It will keep, stored in an airtight container or freezer bag, in the fridge for 3 days or in the freezer for 3 months. Heat through to piping hot to serve.

PANGRATTATO AL POMODORO Ⓥⓔ

Firstly, a confession. This recipe is a twist on an Italian classic, pappa al pomodoro, which is essentially a bread-crust and tomato soup, with olive oil, salt and pepper, and sometimes garlic and basil or rosemary – depending on whose recipe you consider to be sacred. This version eschews the traditional, using dried stuffing crumbs to replace the bread and herbs. But Stuffing Crumb and Tomato Puree Soup didn't seem like a particularly appetizing recipe name, so I translated it into Italian as a nod to the original.

MAKES ENOUGH FOR 3 LITTLE MUGS, OR 1 GENEROUS PORTION

½ small onion

1 tbsp cooking oil

black pepper, to taste

2 medium-sized tomatoes

1 vegetable stock cube

2 tbsp sage and onion stuffing

300–400ml water

30g or 2 tbsp tomato puree

1 tsp light-coloured vinegar, white wine or cider are best but distilled malt vinegar will also work

1 tsp sugar or sweetener of choice

First peel and finely slice your onion and set to one side for a moment.

Measure the oil into a heavy-bottomed saucepan, preferably a non-stick one, and warm it for a moment on a medium heat before adding the onion. Season with a little black pepper and cook for 3–4 minutes, until starting to soften.

Quarter your tomatoes and add those too – when feeling meticulous I confess I cut them into eight apiece, but this may be a step too far for some people.

Crumble over the stock cube, add the stuffing and a splash of the water. Stir well, then add the tomato puree and stir again to incorporate it. Slowly add the remaining water and a scant teaspoon each of vinegar and sugar.

Bring to a simmer, then turn down the heat and continue to cook for around 20 minutes, until the stuffing has swollen and the soup is glossy and thick.

Taste it and adjust the seasoning to your liking before serving.

TO KEEP: This will keep in the fridge for 3 days, or in the freezer for up to 3 months. You may wish to add a splash more liquid if freezing, as I find some dishes go a bit 'thick' in the freezer, so I tend to loosen them a little before storing. Defrost thoroughly and reheat to piping hot throughout to serve.

VEG-PEEL FRITTERS Ⓥ

I use a combination of grated root vegetables and vegetable peelings for these, the ratio varying depending on how much of the latter I have to hand. You can use any mixture of potatoes, sweet potatoes, carrots, parsnips and beetroot – although some of those are naturally grubbier than the others, so proceed with caution! Courgette makes a jolly accompaniment as well – a good variety of colours makes these really rather gorgeous to look at.

SERVES 4

400g mixed root
   vegetables and peels
1 large onion
1 egg
3 tbsp flour
70g cheese, grated
salt and black
   pepper, to taste
oil, for frying

TIP: *Any firm cheese works with these – I've tried blue cheese, crumbly Greek salad cheese and cheap mild Cheddar with great success.*

First, make sure your peels are clean – if they're a bit mucky, bring a pan of water to a vigorous boil, salt it very generously, and drop them in for a minute or two to blanch and loosen the soil. Drain and spread onto a clean, flat tea towel, and rub dry vigorously to remove any stubborn bits. Plunge straight into a bowl of cold water to stop them from cooking any further – you don't want them to be too far gone in comparison to your veg, else the fritters will cook unevenly.

Finely slice your peels, and grate the veg. Then peel and finely chop the onion and place it with the veg and peels into a large mixing bowl.

Crack in the egg and mix well, then add the flour and cheese and mix well to combine. If it needs a hand sticking together, add a tablespoon of cold water and mix again.

Heat a little oil in a frying pan, and add a tablespoon of the fritter mixture. Flatten with the back of a spoon – the thinner they are, the faster they will cook and the crisper they will be. Fry on each side until golden and crisp. Remove from the pan and keep warm.

Repeat until all the fritter mixture has been used. To keep each batch warm as you cook the rest, put them in the oven, heated to the lowest temperature.

I serve these for breakfast with sausages and a poached or fried egg, as a sneaky pile of vegetables and vitamins to start the day, hidden in a tasty Jackson Pollock-esque hot and crispy disguise.

TO KEEP: These freeze brilliantly and can be kept for up to 3 months – you can freeze either the fritter mixture or the cooked fritters. Allow to defrost completely in the fridge for a few hours before cooking or heating through to serve.

CREAM OF MUSHROOM SOUP (Ve)

I love mushroom soup, and I have made many of them over the years, but I think this one is my best so far. If you don't have celery to hand, or don't like it, you can use extra onion. Mushroom soup traditionally has a splash of wine in it, but I try not to keep it in the house at the moment, so if you wanted to add some and it's the kind of thing you have kicking about, do feel free, but I think it's perfectly luxurious and delicious without. This cream is a delicate golden colour – which is a relief from the minky greys of mushroom soups gone by! I use full-fat coconut milk here as you get more bang for your buck, but if you only have the reduced-fat version available, double the quantity and reduce the water accordingly.

SERVES 2

1 small onion
2 celery stalks
4 fat cloves of garlic
1 tbsp cooking oil
300g mushrooms, or thereabouts
1 rounded tbsp flour
1 tsp mixed dried herbs
300ml water
1 vegetable stock cube
200ml coconut milk
plenty of black pepper

Peel and slice your onion as finely as you possibly can. Dice your celery nice and small, and peel and chop your garlic. Warm the oil in a large non-stick pan on a medium heat and add all of these.

Cook on a medium heat for a few minutes to soften, taking care not to let the onions catch or brown. Slice your mushrooms, as thickly or thinly as is personal preference – I prefer some of each in a soup like this one. Add to the pan and stir in for a minute, then add the flour and herbs, and stir quickly to evenly coat the vegetables in a fine dusting of it.

Add a splash of water and mix well and quickly, then add a splash more. It's important to add it a splash at a time so that the flour from the mushrooms forms a roux-style base, rather than a puddle with some floury lumps in, so don't try to rush this step – it's the work of a moment, but it makes all the difference.

When the base liquid is smooth, crumble in your stock cube and add the coconut milk. (The remaining coconut milk should be transferred to a glass or plastic jar, bottle or other container and stored in the fridge.)

Stir well to incorporate the coconut milk and stock, and continue to cook on a low–medium heat for 15 minutes, adding the water gradually until your desired consistency is achieved.

Season with plenty of black pepper to taste; I find the stock makes it quite salty enough for my liking, but you may wish to add a little more. You may serve it as is, or remove half and blend it to smooth, then return it to the pan and stir through – both are excellent.

TO KEEP: Leftovers can be cooled and stored in the fridge for 3 days, or the freezer for 3 months. Some separation is normal when stored in the fridge, simply whisk or beat back together with a wooden spoon to combine when reheating.

TIP: *Keep your eyes peeled in the reduced department of the supermarket or local store for the more exotic mushrooms; I'm not sure about the rest of the country but I seem to find them on a regular basis round my way! Beautiful oyster mushrooms, little rude-looking miniature enokis, big flat portobellos, firm chubby chestnut mushrooms: all have their own subtly different flavours and bring something distinctive to the party. You can slice them and freeze them to use at a later date if you're not going to make this straight away, or if you've already got the oven on fairly low for something, like bread, slice them and pop them on a baking tray on the very bottom to dry them out and store them in an airtight jar for up to 6 months. I say 6 months because I'm a responsible food writer and I don't want to lead any of you into dangerous places, but I must confess I've had my jar of home-dried mushrooms regularly topped up over the last few years, and the ones at the bottom are practically ancient. Do with that information what you will, just keep a keen eye on them and remove any that have any white blooming stuff on the surface if you spot them.*

ROASTED COURGETTE AND RED LENTIL SOUP

Courgettes, when in season, are cheap and abundant, and even when they're not they're still one of the more reasonably priced vegetables for their weight and size. Roasting gives them a lightly smokey, caramelized flavour and dispenses with some of the excess water that they hold, concentrating their often-overlooked qualities into a surprisingly tasty morsel. Red lentils, on the other hand, can be quite dull, so the balsamic vinegar in this recipe does a lot of work in marrying the two together. If you don't have any balsamic, you can use red, white or cider vinegar, with a teaspoon of sugar or sweetener of your choice to replicate the acidity and background sweetness. It won't be exactly the same, but it will be delicious.

MAKES 4 GENEROUS BOWLS

1 tbsp cooking oil
700g courgettes (around 3 medium-sized ones)
1 whole head of garlic
2 large onions, red or white
black pepper, to taste
220g dried red lentils
450ml chicken stock
1 tbsp lemon juice
2 tsp balsamic vinegar

TIP: *Red lentils will hold a lot of water, so check to ensure you do not need to top up your pan; should they start to dry out a little, add an extra splash of water as required.*

Preheat the oven to 190°C/fan 170°C/375°F/gas 5, and make sure there is a shelf in the centre of it. Lightly grease the largest roasting tin that you have that will fit in your oven. Thickly slice the courgettes using the whole vegetable, including the ends, only discarding any particularly tough pieces of the top stalk; the roasting process will pleasantly soften everything, right down to the little button on the bottom.

Quarter your slices and toss into your lightly greased roasting tin. Peel the garlic cloves and add those too. Quarter your onions and peel away the papery outer skin, then place them evenly throughout your roasting tin. Season everything generously with black pepper and roast in the oven for 30 minutes.

Meanwhile, bring a medium pan of unsalted water to the boil and add your red lentils. Once boiling, reduce the heat to a simmer and cover and cook gently for 40 minutes while the courgettes roast.

When your lentils are soft and swollen and your courgettes caramelized and sticky, remove the courgettes from the oven, then drain and thoroughly rinse your lentils under a cold tap. Add both to your blender with the chicken stock, blend until smooth, and then return to your pan. Add the lemon juice and balsamic vinegar and continue to cook on a very low heat for 10 minutes to thicken and reduce. Season to taste with black pepper and a splash more vinegar, if required, and serve hot.

TO KEEP: Allow to cool completely then store in the fridge in food storage bags, clean jars or airtight food-safe containers for up to 3 days. Freeze for up to 3 months. Heat to piping hot to serve.

CHICKEN AND CANNELLINI SOUP

This recipe is just a handful of simple store-cupboard ingredients, but it really is so much more than the sum of its parts. Super easy to throw together, and deliciously comforting. If you don't have cannellini beans to hand, any pale-coloured beans will do: try white kidney beans, chickpeas, butter beans, pinto beans, haricot beans, or even standard cheap baked beans with the tomato sauce rinsed off at a pinch.

SERVES 2

1 x 400g tin of
  cannellini beans
2 chicken stock cubes
1 tbsp lemon juice
plenty of black pepper

Open the tin of cannellini beans and tip the entire contents, including the liquid, into a medium saucepan. Crumble in the stock cube, then fill the tin halfway with cold water and add that too. Add the lemon juice and plenty of black pepper.

Bring to the boil, then reduce to a simmer for 20 minutes, until the beans are very soft.

Decant the contents of the pan into a blender and blend to smooth – or if you prefer a chunky soup, blend half of it and leave half as it is.

Return the blended soup to the pan and simmer for a further 10 minutes to thicken, then serve with more lemon juice and pepper to taste.

TO KEEP: Leftovers will keep in an airtight jar or container in the fridge for up to 3 days, or in the freezer for 6 months. Defrost in the fridge overnight and reheat to piping hot to serve.

CARROT, COCONUT AND CHILLI SOUP

I first made this recipe using frozen chunks of butternut squash, which was delicious, but using carrots makes it far more economical without compromising on the flavour or end result. Should you find yourself in possession of a squash, however, feel free to use that instead in homage to the original. And you may be surprised to know that, as with the carrots, you don't need to peel a squash. The skin is perfectly edible, especially when fried, as here; it adds an almost toffee-flavoured undertone and plenty of fibre into the bargain. I'm almost talking myself into changing this back into a squash recipe, but carrots are cheaper, so carrots it is!

SERVES 4, GENEROUSLY

350g carrots

2 large onions or 250g frozen onion

6 fat cloves of garlic

2 tbsp light cooking oil

a few generous pinches of salt

plenty of black pepper

2 chicken or vegetable stock cubes

700ml water

1 x 400g tin full-fat coconut milk

1 tbsp mixed dried herbs, or dried thyme

½ tsp–1 tsp chilli flakes, to taste

Wash and finely slice your carrots, and peel and slice your onions if using fresh. Peel your garlic cloves and halve them lengthways.

Heat the oil in a large non-stick pan and add all the veg. Season generously with salt and pepper. Fry for a few minutes on a medium heat, stirring to disturb it all so it doesn't stick and burn. Crumble in your stock cubes, and add the water, coconut milk, herbs and chilli. Bring to the boil and reduce to a simmer, for around 20 minutes, until the carrots are very soft.

Transfer everything to a blender and blend until smooth. You may need to do this in batches, depending on the capacity of your blender.

Return the blended soup to the pan and simmer for a further 5–8 minutes to thicken. Serve piping hot.

TO KEEP: Leftovers will keep in the fridge for 3 days, or in the freezer for up to 6 months. Defrost thoroughly in the fridge overnight and reheat to piping hot to serve.

CHICKEN PORRIDGE
WITH A POACHED EGG

This is a savoury twist on classic porridge, and although it might sound a little unusual, savoury oatmeal is something that's enjoyed worldwide, even if it hasn't quite caught on in the UK yet. I'm on a bit of a fervent mission to change that; a version of this recipe first appeared in *Good Food For Bad Days*, using a skin-on chicken thigh for ultimate comfort food. This version is simpler, and slightly cheaper, and the egg poached into it is the perfect finishing touch.

SERVES 1

1 chicken stock cube

40g porridge oats

400ml milk – ordinary or coconut are both fine

1 egg

a pinch of salt and plenty of black pepper

First crumble your chicken stock cube into a medium saucepan, then add the oats and milk. Place on a low heat and simmer gently, stirring continuously. Don't allow the milk to boil over; if it threatens to, simply swiftly remove it from the heat and allow it to settle, before cautiously heating it again.

When the porridge is thick and creamy, make a little dent in the centre, like a well. Crack the egg into the well, then cover with a lid and continue to warm through for a minute or two. Remove the porridge from the heat, and keep covered for 2–3 minutes longer, so the egg continues to cook in the residual heat from the pan.

Season with salt and pepper and enjoy immediately.

RADISH, SOFT CHEESE AND LENTIL SALAD ⓥ

Radishes are routinely one of the cheapest salad vegetables available in the supermarket, and in my opinion are also criminally underrated. This is one of my favourite ways to enjoy them. (The other is simply dunked in the anchovy mayonnaise on page 56, over and over again.)

SERVES 2 AS A MAIN MEAL OR 4 AS A SIDE

2 tbsp light cooking oil

20ml light-coloured vinegar

½ tsp mixed dried herbs

a generous pinch of salt

plenty of black pepper

1 x 400g tin brown or green lentils

100g radishes

¼ cucumber

75g soft cream cheese

4 tbsp mayonnaise

100g or thereabouts mixed young salad leaves

a handful of fresh basil, mint or parsley

First dress your lentils. Measure the oil and vinegar into a bowl, and add the herbs, salt and pepper. Whisk well with a fork to combine. Drain your lentils and rinse them thoroughly, then add to the dressing and mix well to coat them. Stand this to one side for a moment.

Very finely slice your radishes and cucumber – if you have a mandolin slicer, this is an ideal use for it, but if not, a very sharp small knife will do. Add these to the lentils and fold through so that they, too, benefit from the delicious dressing.

In a separate small bowl, beat together the cream cheese and mayonnaise, along with a little more pepper.

Add the salad leaves and herbs immediately before serving, and give everything one last toss to mix it all up. Dollop the cream cheese–mayo mixture on top and enjoy immediately.

TO KEEP: This will keep in the fridge for a day and a night, or a night and a day, but any longer than that and the salad leaves may start to go a bit limp and not as enjoyable. If you hold off with the leaves and just add them to your bowl before serving instead of to the entire dish, the radish and lentil mixture will keep for up to 3 days, covered, in the fridge.

LEMON SARDINES ON TOAST

Those of my readers who follow me on Twitter or Instagram will no doubt be aware of my longstanding, loud and loquacious love affair with tinned sardines; I often joke that my ideal Advent calendar would consist of twenty-four different varieties, and one day perhaps I'll even be organized enough to make myself one. Until that blessed day, here's one of my favourite ways to enjoy them: quickly, simply, cheaply and nutritiously, all admirable qualities in such a regular meal.

SERVES 1

1 x 120g tin of
  sardines in oil
1 thick slice of bread
  – the end of the loaf
  is perfect here
1 tbsp lemon juice
plenty of black pepper

Carefully remove your sardines from the tin, reserving the oil, and set them to one side for a moment. Pop your bread on to toast.

Heat the oil from the sardine tin in a frying pan on a medium heat until it is very hot but not smoking, then carefully add your sardines. They may spit a little when they embrace the hot pan, so be cautious!

Fry the sardines for a couple of minutes on one side, turn them over and add the lemon juice, then fry for a couple of minutes on the other side, until the skin is crisp.

Place the toasted bread on a plate and place the sardines on top. Add the juices from the pan, and season generously with pepper. Enjoy immediately.

TO KEEP: Tinned sardines have an unfortunate habit of permeating everything they possibly can in the fridge, so should you have any leftovers, pop them in a clean jar with a splash of oil, a clean recycled margarine tub, or a very tightly rolled freezer bag to keep them to themselves. Enjoy within 2 days of cooking, either cold or warmed through, or mix well with a generous dollop of mayo to make a spreadable pate-type-thing that will keep for up to a week in a clean, tightly lidded jar.

BEANS, PULSES AND LENTILS

Beans, pulses and lentils have been a bedrock of my cookery ever since my first forays into recipe writing, cobbling together staples from the local food bank with whatever the cheapest goods at the nearest supermarket were at the time. They are an incredibly cheap, varied and versatile source of protein, which can be used to stretch out meat dishes, as a partial or complete substitute for mince, a thickener for soups and stews, blended into dips, tossed with dressings to make a speedy salad, or taking centre stage in a dinner in their own right. They are also largely interchangeable, so although each has their own qualities and attributes, if you don't have one to hand or don't particularly like a certain kind, feel free to swap it out for something similar.

Dried beans are cheaper than the tinned variety — because as with everything in today's society, you pay a premium for the slightest convenience — but they do require soaking overnight before using. If you like to meal plan and can afford a little extra fuel to cook them with, then by all means stock up on the dried varieties, but for ease and consistency I have written the recipes that follow as though with tinned beans. The exception to this rule is the lentils, which don't need soaking and cook very quickly from dried.

If using dried beans, the general rule is that they double in volume and weight when soaked overnight, so where a recipe specifies 1 x 400g tin, the drained weight is around 240g, so the dried equivalent would be 120g plus thrice the volume of water. A pinch of baking powder or bicarbonate of soda in the soaking water helps them to soften, and never add salt whilst soaking nor cooking, as it causes the skins to 'seize' and your beans to frustratingly never quite soften. Season at the end of the cooking time, to taste.

GARLIC BREAD RIBOLLITA

An excellent way to use up leftover garlic bread, or any crusty or stale bread that you have kicking about the place, and transform it into a hearty, healthy meal suitable for almost any time of day. I say almost but I have been known to crack an egg into leftover ribollita, poach it, and scoff it for breakfast. So it really is that versatile.

SERVES 4

1 onion

4 celery stalks

1 large or 2 small
   carrots, washed if they
   are a bit grubby

2 fat or 4 small
   cloves of garlic

2 tbsp light cooking oil

a pinch of chilli

1 tsp mixed dried herbs

1 chicken or vegetable
   stock cube

1 x 400g tin of plum or
   chopped tomatoes

1 x 400g tin of borlotti,
   pinto or cannellini
   beans, or baked beans
   with the sauce rinsed off

2 tsp light-coloured
   vinegar or bottled
   lemon juice

150g garlic bread
   (or other bread)

a little hard strong
   cheese, grated

plenty of black pepper

200g spring greens,
   or kale, finely sliced,
   or frozen spinach

Peel and finely slice your onion and chop the celery. Finely slice your carrots, there's no need to peel them. Peel the garlic and halve it lengthways, and set everything to one side for a moment.

Heat your oil in a large non-stick pan and add the chopped veg and garlic. Fry on a medium heat for around 5 minutes, stirring every now and then to disturb them a little.

Add the chilli and herbs and crumble over the stock cube, then pour over the tomatoes and the beans, including their liquid – it adds a rich texture and helps to thicken the overall finished ribollita. I do this with most beans, except kidney beans, these days. Add 300ml cold water, which is roughly the volume of one of your empty tins, and the vinegar or lemon juice. Bring to the boil, mashing the tomatoes with a fork, wooden spoon or spatula, then reduce to a simmer.

Dice your garlic bread and add to the pan, along with most of the cheese, and plenty of black pepper. Simmer on a medium heat for 25 minutes, topping up with a splash more water if necessary – not all hobs nor pans were created equal, so the likelihood of needing a little extra water is infinitely variable.

Finely slice your greens, if using fresh ones, or simply toss them in if using frozen ones, around 4 minutes before the end of the cooking time. Serve immediately, topped with the remaining cheese and plenty more pepper, or warm through if made in advance.

TO KEEP: This will keep in the fridge, tightly covered or in a food-safe bag or airtight container, for up to 3 days, or in the freezer for up to 3 months. Defrost thoroughly and reheat to piping hot to serve.

VEG-PEEL FALAFELS ⓥ

Save the peels from your vegetables when preparing a roast dinner, pop them in a freezer bag or airtight container in the fridge, and use them to bolster these tiny tasty morsels. I use non-organic vegetables, so I give them a good scrub before peeling, making them perfectly safe to eat. You can use the scrubbed peelings from potatoes, parsnips, carrots, the outer layer of leeks and onions, celery leaves and any outer leaves of cabbages – pretty much any scrappy veg bits will do!

SERVES 4 (6 PER PORTION)

150g vegetable peelings and scraps

cooking oil, for frying and greasing

a pinch or two of salt

1 tbsp medium curry powder

1 x 400g tin of cooked chickpeas, plus 2 tbsp aquafaba

2 tbsp gram or besan flour, or plain flour

TIP: *'Aquafaba' may sound like a fancy ingredient, but it's simply the gloopy liquid from a tin of chickpeas or other cooked beans. It's used here to help bind the falafel mixture to stop it from crumbling.*

First, finely chop your veg peelings – you want them to be as inconspicuous as possible. Use a large sharp knife to finely slice them, then chop to smithereens or pop them in a food processor or bullet blender and pulse for a minute until shredded.

Heat 1 tablespoon of oil in a large non-stick pan and add the veg, along with the salt. Cook for around 4 minutes to soften, then add the curry powder, and stir it in to coat the veg.

Drain the chickpeas, reserving the liquid in a jug or bowl. Add the chickpeas to the pan, along with 1 tablespoon of the reserved liquid, and mash until pulpy. Add another tablespoon of aquafaba and mash again. Remove from the heat and stir in the flour, then transfer to a container to cool. Chill in the fridge for 4 hours, or overnight.

When the mixture is chilled and firm, remove it from the fridge. Lightly oil your hands. Pinch off a walnut-sized piece and shape it into a ball with your hands, pressing firmly with your palms to bring it back together if it cracks. Repeat until all of the mixture has been formed into balls.

Heat 2.5cm of oil in a small deep saucepan on the smallest hob ring, until it starts to bubble. Turn down the heat and carefully place a few of the falafels in using a slotted spoon: do NOT just drop them in as you may splash yourself with boiling oil! Cook for 2–3 minutes, then gently turn them over to cook the other side. Remove with the slotted spoon and place them in a bowl, and repeat until they are all cooked. If the cooking starts to slow down or they aren't going as golden as quickly, briefly turn the heat back up until the oil starts to bubble again, then turn it down again. Never leave boiling oil unattended, and never leave it on a high heat as it can catch fire.

When the falafels are all cooked, you can eat them immediately, at room temperature, or straight from the fridge as a snack.

TO KEEP: They will keep for 3 days in the fridge or 3 months in the freezer. You can also freeze the uncooked mixture, but defrost it completely and allow it to come to room temperature before shaping and frying.

RED LENTIL AND ONION DIP (Ve)

A delicious and enjoyable way to sneak in some veggies, using just a handful of simple store-cupboard and basic ingredients. I feel compelled to warn you that I idly polished off this entire bowl in one afternoon of writing and recipe testing, so the idea that it serves four is a guideline only, but one to which I struggled to personally adhere!

MAKES 4 X 100G PORTIONS

100g dried red lentils

1 medium onion, approx 100g

2 medium carrots, approx 100g

2 tbsp light cooking oil

a pinch each of salt and black pepper

1 vegetable stock cube

1 fat or 2 small cloves of garlic

To serve

2 white or wholemeal flatbreads or pitta breads

vegetable crudités

First, thoroughly rinse your lentils under cold running water to remove any residue. Then pop them in a saucepan that will easily hold several times their volume, and cover with 400ml cold water. Place on a medium hob ring on a high heat and bring to the boil, then reduce to a simmer and leave them to soften. This will take around 20 minutes.

While your lentils are cooking, peel your onion and chop it very finely. Coarsely grate your carrots; you can leave the skin on here and use the entire carrot for this recipe, including the gnarly top bit as far as you are able to grate it.

Heat the oil in a non-stick saucepan or frying pan, and add the carrot and onion. Season with salt and fry on a high heat for a minute, stirring to disturb it so it doesn't stick and burn. Then turn the heat down as low as it will go. Crumble over the stock cube and stir it into the veg, then leave them to soften as the lentils cook, stirring intermittently.

When the lentils have absorbed all of the water and are very soft, pour them into the pan with the carrot and onion. Peel your garlic and finely grate it into the pan, and stir into the mixture for a minute.

Turn the heat back up to high for a minute so the mixture thickens; it should be the consistency and texture of a rough hummus. Add more oil to thin to your desired taste, and season with salt and pepper to finish.

Serve with flatbreads, pitta or vegetable crudités, and enjoy warm or chilled.

TO KEEP: This dip will keep in the fridge, covered or stored in an airtight container or food storage bag, for up to 3 days.

KIDNEY BEAN
AND PINEAPPLE CURRY (Ve)

The combination of fruit and beans may sound an odd one, but this recipe is based loosely on the most popular dish on my website, the peach and chickpea curry from *A Girl Called Jack*. Encouraged by a decade of enthusiasm and delighted surprise from my lovely readers, I set out to make a new variation that would be just as good, and dare I even suggest it, but I think this one hits that spot. If you have a blender, blend half of the pineapple with the chopped tomatoes to make a sweet-sour sauce base, but if you don't have one, or don't want the hassle of cleaning it, it's just as delicious cooked whole and hearty instead.

SERVES 4

1 large onion, or
   140g frozen onions

1 tbsp cooking oil,
   any kind

a generous pinch of salt

4 fat cloves of garlic

1cm piece of fresh
   root ginger

2 tbsp medium
   curry powder

1 x 540g tin of
   pineapple chunks

1 x 400g tin of
   kidney beans

2 x 400g tins of
   chopped tomatoes

black pepper

First peel and dice your onion, if using a fresh one, and place it in a large non-stick pan. If you're using frozen onions, simply tip them in. Add the oil, and a generous pinch of salt, and cook for 5 minutes on a medium heat to start to soften.

Peel the garlic and chop finely, along with the ginger, and stir in well, then spoon in the curry powder. Pour in the pineapple, along with all of the juice (if you're using pineapple in syrup, tip in around a quarter of the liquid, any more and it may be too sweet). Drain and rinse the kidney beans thoroughly and add those too, then cover with the tomatoes and stir well to combine. Season generously with black pepper, and simmer for 30 minutes, stirring occasionally to prevent it from sticking and burning. You may need to add a splash of water to stop the pan from drying out – this is not an exact science, as all tins of fruit and tomatoes tend to have slightly different liquid contents, so keep an eye on it and adjust it to suit.

When the curry is ready, remove from the heat and serve.

TO KEEP: This is a dish that improves with age (to a point!) so leftovers the next day are even more delicious as the flavours develop further as it cools. Keep in an airtight container, covered bowl, or food storage bag in the fridge for up to 3 days, or in the freezer for 3 months.

OLD REJUVENATED BREAD WITH CHICKPEAS AND GREENS

This is a quick and tasty dish that can be enjoyed on its own or as a side to a larger meal. You can make the garlic paste ahead of time and freeze it in ice cube trays – simply put a bulb of garlic into a food processor with a touch of water and blend it to a paste (you can do the same with the fresh root ginger).

SERVES 4

1 garlic clove or
   2 tbsp garlic paste

2cm piece of fresh root
   ginger, peeled

100g bread (any
   bread will do)

4 tbsp olive oil (or
   vegetable, sunflower
   or rapeseed oil)

1 x 400g tin chickpeas
   or cannellini beans,
   drained and rinsed (any
   tinned beans will do)

1 tbsp ground paprika

1 tbsp ground cumin

½ tsp ground turmeric

150g frozen spinach,
   defrosted and drained
   (or fresh or tinned,
   or chopped kale)

1 chicken or vegetable
   stock cube

salt and freshly ground
   black pepper

1 tbsp lemon juice, to serve

First peel and grate or finely chop your garlic, and grate or finely chop your ginger, and set to one side for a moment. Dice your bread into small pieces, and set those aside too.

Heat the oil in a large frying pan for half a minute or until it starts to sizzle gently. Add the chickpeas, reserving the liquid from the tin to use in a moment. Add the garlic, ginger, paprika, cumin and turmeric and fry on a medium heat for 3–4 minutes, then tip in the liquid from the chickpea tin.

Add the bread and spinach and stir well to combine. Crumble in the stock cube, add a splash of water if needed, season with salt and pepper, and bring to the boil. Reduce the heat and simmer for 15 minutes, until the bread is soft and swollen and the chickpeas are super tender.

Squeeze in the lemon juice just before serving either hot or cold, with a little more pepper to make it really sing.

TO KEEP: Will keep in the fridge for 3 days but it is not recommended for freezing as it can fall victim to 'freezer burn', due to the lack of sauce element.

BLACK PUDDING AND LENTIL RAGU

Green lentils don't technically need to be soaked before cooking, as they will get tender with a 30-minute simmer, so if you don't have time or didn't plan ahead, all is not lost. But if you do fancy being organized, knock a good 10–12 minutes off the simmer time, and your energy bill, by soaking your lentils in cold water overnight.

SERVES 4

120g dried green or
   brown lentils

1 large onion or
   2 small ones

4 generous celery stalks

1 large carrot

1 tbsp cooking oil

120g black pudding

salt and black pepper

4 fat cloves of garlic

1 x 400g tin of tomatoes

300ml chicken, veg
   or beef stock

1 tsp mixed dried herbs
   or fresh thyme leaves

a dash of light-
   coloured vinegar

Pop the dried lentils into a bowl, jug or pan that will easily hold thrice their volume, and cover with cold water. You'll need double the volume of water to lentils, and then some. Leave them to soak for at least 8 hours, or overnight, in a reasonably cool place in the kitchen.

When the time comes to cook them, drain the lentils and rinse thoroughly in a sieve under cold running water. Transfer them to a saucepan that will hold twice their volume, and cover with fresh cold water. Don't salt it (see Tip). Bring to the boil then reduce to a low simmer, covered if possible, while you prepare the ragu.

Halve and then finely dice your onion, then finely slice the celery and dice or grate the carrot. Heat the oil in a large non-stick pan and add the prepared vegetables. Roughly chop the black pudding and add that too. Season with salt and pepper and fry over a medium heat for around 10 minutes. Give them a stir every now and then to cook them evenly and prevent them sticking and burning.

Peel and finely slice or roughly chop your garlic, and add that to the pan. Drain and thoroughly rinse the lentils, and pour them in, followed by the tomatoes and the stock. Add the herbs, a dash of vinegar, and a little more black pepper. Bring to the boil, then cover and reduce to a simmer. Simmer for 25 minutes until the lentils are very soft and the black pudding has all but melted into the ragu. Taste and adjust the seasoning as preferred, and serve over piping hot mash or your favourite pasta.

TO KEEP: Store in an airtight container, jar or food storage bag in the fridge for up to 3 days, or freezer for up to 3 months. Defrost thoroughly and reheat to piping hot to serve.

TIP: *When cooking lentils, don't add salt to the water as the skins will seize and harden and you'll be cooking them forever trying to coax them to soften up again. But you could add a few pinches of bicarbonate of soda or baking powder if you have some kicking about; it really softens them up. And do give them a thorough rinse before cooking; it removes the residue that forms a foamy layer in the pan rather like the scum at the edge of the tide – not harmful, but not particularly appetizing! Soaking and rinsing well also helps to reduce the, erm, 'gaseous after-effects' of introducing beans and pulses to your diet – so it's worth a little forward planning for a few quid off the energy bill AND a slightly more harmonious household.*

MANDARIN, WHITE BEAN
AND GREEK CHEESE SALAD ⓥ

This simple salad can be served as a side dish at a barbecue or as a filling lunch in its own right. The combination may sound a little odd, but trust me – it really works! I tend to keep a pot of these pickled beans in my fridge always now; they're an excellent little snack at any time of day, and the flavour improves with a rest. The soft, salty tang of feta (or 'Greek-style salad cheese', as it is known in some supermarket budget ranges) pairs perfectly with the sweet and juicy mandarins and creamy beans, but you could swap it out for a cheap blue cheese, or most supermarkets sell a budget brie that would work here too. (Or at least they did at the time of writing this, and I'll feel proper daft if that changes in the six months between handing in the book manuscript and getting it onto the shelves!)

SERVES 4

For the beans

2 x 400g tins of any combination of cannellini, borlotti, chickpea, haricot or pinto beans

1 small onion

6 fat cloves of garlic

1 tsp mixed dried herbs

75ml light-coloured vinegar

½ tsp salt

plenty of black pepper

150ml light cooking oil

For the salad

1 x 298g tin of mandarin segments in juice

100ml light-coloured vinegar

100ml oil

100g mixed salad leaves

a handful of fresh parsley

a handful of fresh basil

100g feta or other Greek-style salad cheese

The pickled beans will need to be made well in advance of the salad – they start to come into their own around 4 days after bottling, so this recipe takes some planning, but it is worth the wait!

First, thoroughly rinse and drain the beans, and transfer to a large mixing bowl. Peel and very finely slice your onion, and peel and roughly chop the garlic, then add those to the beans. Measure in the dried herbs and mix everything together briefly. Set it all to one side for a moment.

Choose a saucepan or cooking pot that will easily hold double the volume of the contents of your mixing bowl. Measure in the vinegar, salt and pepper, and place on a medium hob ring on a high heat. Bring to the boil, then reduce to a simmer. Add the beans mixture, then pour over the oil and continue to simmer for 4 or 5 more minutes, keeping a watchful eye on it as boiling oil should never be left unattended.

Meanwhile, wash and rinse your jars and lids, and pop them on a baking sheet in a low oven, around 120°C/fan 100°C/250°F/gas ½ will do. Heat them for 10 minutes to sterilize them, then turn the oven off – without opening it – until you need the jars.

Remove the pan from the heat and stir the contents together well, as the oil will be sitting on top of the other ingredients. Ladle evenly into the clean, sterilized jars, filling to the neck to create an airtight seal. Fasten the lids immediately, and leave to cool completely before transferring to the fridge. Gently turn the jars a few times at least once a day to redistribute the ingredients, before returning to the fridge.

To make the salad, strain the mandarins through a fine-mesh sieve set over a jug or mixing bowl to separate the juice from the fruit. Pour the juice into a jar or bottle with a tight-fitting lid and the light-coloured vinegar and oil. Add a few pinches of salt and some pepper, and seal the vessel tightly. Shake well to emulsify and make the dressing, and set it to one side.

Add the salad leaves to a large mixing bowl. Chop the parsley and add most of this to the leaves along with most of the whole basil leaves. Using a slotted spoon, add a generous amount of the pickled beans, then add the drained mandarins, and crumble in the feta. Dress generously with the mandarin dressing and toss briefly to coat everything. Serve with more black pepper to taste, and garnish with the remaining herbs.

TO KEEP: The beans will keep for 2 months in the fridge unopened in their jar, but use within a week of opening and keep them stored in the fridge for this time. I like to make several smaller jars so I can keep a stash going for longer. The salad dressing will keep in the fridge for up to 10 days – just shake it every few days to re-combine it and it will last a bit longer.

LENTIL KEEMA ⓥ

Keema is traditionally made with lamb, but this lentil version more than holds its own, and for a fraction of the cost. If your budget stretches to butter, a tablespoon or two stirred through at the very end of the cooking process makes this dish utterly delectable, but if not, it's perfectly fine without.

SERVES 4

120g dried brown
  or green lentils

1 large onion

8–10 fat cloves of garlic

20g fresh root ginger

a handful of fresh mint
  and coriander

½ tsp chilli flakes or
  ¼ tsp chilli powder

2 tbsp light cooking oil

a pinch or two of salt

1 tbsp cumin, seeds
  or ground

1 tbsp ground coriander

1 tbsp ground turmeric

100g natural yoghurt

1 tbsp flour (optional)

100g frozen peas

Place your lentils in a large saucepan and cover with cold, unsalted water. Bring to the boil, then reduce to a simmer. Cover and simmer for 20 minutes. (You can soak them first to reduce the cooking time if you have time – see page 88.)

Meanwhile, peel and finely slice your onion. Place half in a blender or food processor, and set half to one side to use in a moment.

Peel the garlic and add to the blender, then roughly chop your ginger and add that too. Add most of the mint and coriander, including the soft stalks and discarding any tough mint stalks. Set aside the remainder. Add the chilli, and 1 tablespoon each of oil and water, then blend to a smooth paste.

Heat 1 tablespoon of oil in a large non-stick pan and add the reserved finely sliced onion and a pinch or two of salt. Fry on a medium heat for 2–3 minutes to start to soften, then add the cumin, coriander and turmeric. Stir for a minute to coat the onion in the spices, then pour over the paste from the blender and stir in slowly and gently. Turn the heat down very low, and let it cook gently.

Measure the yoghurt into a bowl, and add 1 tablespoon of the hot paste mixture. Stir in well, then repeat. Repeat this step until your yoghurt has doubled in volume and is warm to the touch, then tip the whole lot back into the saucepan and stir through. This brings the yoghurt gently to temperature, which should stop it splitting and separating, but if it does separate a little, simply add a tablespoon of flour and beat it briskly to bring it back together again, then thin with a little water and beat some more until it is well combined.

When your lentils are soft, thoroughly drain and rinse them, and add to the sauce. Mix well and cook for a further 10 minutes. Add the frozen peas a minute or two before serving, and garnish with the reserved fresh coriander and mint.

TO KEEP: Store in an airtight container, jar or food storage bag in the fridge for up to 3 days, or freezer for up to 3 months. Defrost thoroughly and reheat to piping hot to serve.

AN EXTRA HELPING

I like to serve this lentil keema with soft white rolls, reminiscent of a favourite breakfast I once had at the Dishoom restaurant in Edinburgh, where I was caught by an amused waiter stuffing leftovers into a little buttery bun and wrapping it in a napkin 'for later on'. They were far more amused when I promised to bring the napkin back, and actually did!

Although a trip to the other side of the country isn't an essential component part of this recipe, should you find yourself in the vicinity with the means to treat yourself to the best breakfast in town, there's very little as wholesome and lovely as climbing to the top of Arthur's Seat or the foot of Edinburgh Castle, slipping a hand in a pocket and finding a slightly squashed, spicy, buttery bun to nibble as you admire the view. But maybe take your own piece of kitchen roll with you; I don't want to suddenly find myself responsible for a linen shortage in the Scottish hospitality industry . . .

BUTTER BEAN, VEG AND STUFFING STEW

It's no secret that I'm a fan of cheap packet stuffing for all manner of culinary surprises – from a crispy coating for chicken nuggets to a topping for mac 'n' cheese, to folding it into a bread dough for little herby surprises. The uses I have found for it over the years are so numerous that I constantly have a ready supply of the cheapest boxes decanted into a 1-litre airtight jar on the kitchen shelf, with instructions written on the side in black marker as to how many grams per millilitre of water to make up standard stuffing. I nestle the jar between the salt and turmeric, with equal gravitas to both. My favourite incarnation is to use it as a thickener to soups and stews that need a little bit of a lift, like this one, rustled together from frozen veg, a couple of tins, and whatever is rolling around in purgatory at the bottom of the fridge. You could add greens to this, if you have them, or some pasta to make this a more substantial meal that riffs somewhere between a minestrone and a ribollita, while being rather like neither at all.

SERVES 4

1 large onion, or 150g frozen onion

6 fat cloves of garlic

1 tbsp cooking oil

a pinch of salt and pepper

1 large carrot or two tiddlers

1 x 400g tin of butter beans

500ml chicken or vegetable stock (see page 218 for homemade)

1 x 400g tin of plum or chopped tomatoes

1 tbsp lemon juice or light-coloured vinegar

1 tsp sweet paprika

1 large courgette

4 tbsp dried stuffing crumbs

First peel and finely dice your onion, and toss it into a large non-stick pan. If you're using frozen onions, simply measure them in.

Peel your garlic, halve each clove lengthways and toss them in too. Measure in the oil, add a pinch of salt and pepper, and bring to a low heat to start to soften. Very finely dice the carrot and add to the pan, and give everything a good stir. Cook all together for 5 minutes, just to knock the acerbic edge off the alliums.

Drain and thoroughly rinse the butter beans and tip into the pan, then cover with first the stock, then the tomatoes. Bring to the boil, then reduce to a simmer. Measure in the lemon juice or vinegar and paprika, and cook for 40 minutes until the veg and beans are super soft and the liquid is reduced and thickened.

Finely slice the courgette so the slices are almost translucent; they will disappear into the stew in a rather pleasing manner. Add to the pan along with the stuffing and cook for a further 10 minutes, stirring occasionally to combine. Season with a little extra salt and pepper to taste, and serve warm.

TO KEEP: This will keep for up to 3 days in the fridge, or 3 months in the freezer.

TIP: *I must admit to loving a frozen onion for the speed and simplicity of having them to hand, and am using them more and more these days. I've done the cost calculation and frozen onions work out – at the time of writing, which is ever subject to change – at 0.18p per gram, whereas fresh work out at 0.09p per gram. So they are ever so slightly more expensive than buying the cheapest fresh ones at the supermarket – but with frozen you only use what you need, and there is no waste from the skins and outer layer.*

POTATOES

Potatoes are that glorious combination of being both incredibly cheap all year round and incredibly versatile in innumerable delicious ways, making them a key part of many a thrifty home cook's regular repertoire. The culinary jury tends to be somewhat divided over where the best place to store them is, but I've found that they last a great deal longer in the fridge than in a cool dark cupboard. If your fridge space is at a premium, however, the cupboard is just fine.

REFRIED ROAST POTATOES
WITH BLUE CHEESE ⓥ

These refried roast potatoes work as a cross between a warm potato salad and a potato hash, so use any leftover veg and cheese you have kicking around, the recipe is a suggestion only but it's my fave combination! Vegetarians and vegans, feel free to use your fave plant-based equivalent for the bacon and cheese – there are loads of brilliant alternatives available!

SERVES 2, ALLEGEDLY

50g blue cheese
100ml mayonnaise
1 small leek or onion
100g cooking or
    streaky bacon
6–8 leftover roast potatoes
1 large or 2 small apples
2 tbsp cooking oil
a pinch of salt
plenty of black pepper

First make your dressing by chopping the blue cheese into small pieces and adding to a bowl along with the mayonnaise. Mash the cheese well with a fork and beat together until smooth and well combined. Set to one side. It may seem a little thick but it loosens when added to the hot potatoes later!

Finely slice your leek or onion, and roughly chop the bacon. Cut each roast potato into approximately six pieces. Dice the apples and set everything aside for a moment.

Heat the oil in a non-stick, shallow pan and add the bacon. Fry for a minute, then add the potatoes and season with a pinch of salt. Fry those for a minute or two, then add the leeks. Cook everything together, stirring a few times to crisp everything evenly and prevent anything from sticking and burning, for around 5 minutes. Serve with the dressing dolloped over the top, with plenty of black pepper to finish. Best eaten straight away.

TO KEEP: Leftovers (leftovers?!) will keep in the fridge for up to 2 days, covered well, and can be enjoyed cold. I'd be wary of reheating them again, seeing as they've been cooked once as roast potatoes and then again for this recipe, but trust me, this is as delicious as a cold potato salad as it as a warm one.

BASIC POTATO SALAD (V)

You could skip the first two and a half steps of this recipe by buying tinned potatoes and save the energy cost and effort of cooking them, as they are cooked to perfection – just soft enough and just firm enough; simply halve them and pick the recipe up from 'peel and halve your onion'. (Bizarrely, at the time of writing this book and for the decade previously, tinned cooked potatoes have worked out cheaper per gram than the cheapest fresh ones in the same supermarket – they tend to be the tiddlers that don't make the weight grade for the pre-packed bags or loose selection.)

SERVES 2–4

400g potatoes, any kind

a generous few
    pinches of salt

1 small onion

a handful of fresh
    soft herbs

3 tbsp mayonnaise

1 tsp English mustard

1 tbsp cooking oil

1 tbsp light-coloured
    vinegar

plenty of black pepper

First scrub your potatoes, leaving the skins on but taking care to clean them thoroughly. I use a designated nail brush for vegetables, as it's cheaper than buying a veg brush and easy to keep clean and hygienic – make sure you clearly label it as being just for vegetables! Dice into 2.5cm chunks, and pop into a large saucepan. Cover with cold water and a few generous pinches of salt and bring to the boil. Reduce to a simmer for around 15 minutes, or until the potatoes are soft but not falling apart.

While the potatoes are simmering, peel and halve your onion, then slice it very finely. Set to one side for a moment. Very finely chop your herbs, including any soft stalks, and set those aside too.

Drain your potatoes and give them a quick spritz under the cold tap to prevent them cooking any further, then return them to the pan to save you a bit of washing up. Add the onion and most of the herbs to the potatoes.

Grab a small bowl, jug, or mug and spoon in the mayo and mustard. Add the oil and vinegar a teaspoon at a time – 3 teaspoons – and beat well into the mayo and mustard to combine before adding the next. Some shop-bought mayo can be temperamental with vinegars, so adding it slowly and combining it briskly helps to prevent it from splitting – which if it does happen doesn't look brilliant but will still taste absolutely fine, so don't worry too much if you don't get this right first time.

Add the sauce to the pan, and gently mix it with the onions and potatoes to coat them. Finish with the remaining herbs and plenty of black pepper to taste.

TO KEEP: This will keep for up to 3 days in the fridge, well covered or in an airtight container, lidded jar or food storage bag. Not recommended for freezing.

POTATO, PARSLEY AND ANCHOVY SALAD

This very simple recipe is easy to knock together in a matter of minutes; ideal for unexpected lunch guests or a quick treat for yourself. The tinned potatoes are already cooked, and the strong flavours of the anchovies and the freshness of the parsley will help to mitigate any suspicions you may have about using them in the first place.

SERVES 1 GENEROUSLY OR 2 LIGHTLY

1 small onion
6 anchovy fillets
1 tbsp bottled lemon juice
3 tbsp light cooking oil
a pinch of salt
plenty of black pepper
a pinch of chilli flakes, plus extra
1 x 540g tin of potatoes
a fistful of fresh parsley

First, peel and very finely slice your onion, then set it to one side.

Next, make the dressing. Drain and roughly chop the anchovies and pop them into a small clean jar with a lid. Add the lemon juice and oil, salt, pepper and chilli, and screw the lid on tight. Shake well to combine and set to one side.

Drain your potatoes and halve them lengthways – quarter any particularly large ones. Pop them into a microwave-safe bowl and warm through for 2 minutes.

While the potatoes are warming, finely chop your parsley, including the stalks, and set to one side.

Remove the potatoes carefully from the microwave and toss in the dressing, making sure to scrape all of the anchovies out of the jar. Finish with liberal amounts of the parsley and a little extra chilli and pepper, then serve.

TO KEEP: Best enjoyed immediately, but it will keep in the fridge, well covered, for up to 3 days. Not recommended for freezing. Leftovers can be enjoyed warm or cold.

INSTANT MOONSHINE MASH WITH VEG AND BACON JUMBLE

Moonshine Mash first appeared in *Cooking On A Bootstrap*, a bootleg riff on polenta made with potatoes and corn. I so-named it because 'hooch', or moonshine, is typically made from potatoes or corn, and the idea of my own sneaky, irreverent take on something usually considered, well, a bit sneaky and irreverent in itself rather tickled me. This version takes the idea even further into the depths of culinary depravity, firstly by blending tinned corn and its brine, with milk, to create a 'corn milk' – not dissimilar to the 'carrot milk' theory in the carrot cake oats in *Tin Can Cook* that equally delighted and horrified viewers of *Daily Kitchen Live* when I demonstrated it in lockdown. I then add instant mash, the cheapest available variety, to this corn milk abomination and you know what? It works really well. My son, who can be a frustratingly fussy eater at times, absolutely loved it. The corn gives an underlying sweetness, the skins that get stuck in our teeth are blitzed away to a much more manageable nothing, and the additional flavour bolsters and enhances the usually plain and laggy texture of instant mash to something genuinely luxurious. I opted not to add fat to mine, but you could enrich it with butter or a splash of good oil, if you like.

SERVES 2

4 sausages

200ml milk

1 vegetable stock cube (optional)

120g tinned sweetcorn

80g broccoli stalk

140g carrot

100g onion

1 tbsp lard or oil

salt and black pepper

50g bacon

20g instant gravy granules

1 cup of boiling water

48g dried instant mash

8g hard, strong, dried grated cheese

Fry the sausages in a griddle pan or frying pan on the hob for around 15 minutes, piercing carefully with a fork two or three times to ensure they cook through. Cheap sausages tend to be fatty enough to not need any extra lubrication, but if you do feel the need, you can add a splash of oil or a nub of lard or other fat to get them going.

Measure the milk into a blender – I use a small bullet blender – and add 100ml water and the stock cube, if using. Add the sweetcorn – this may sound incredibly slovenly but I don't bother to drain it these days, a little brine isn't going to do any harm here. Blend thoroughly to a smooth, buttersoft yellow liquid. Pour it into a saucepan and leave it there for a moment.

Transfer your attention to your vegetables. To make these tiny mirepoix-style small and delicate pieces, I first slice the broccoli stalk, carrot and onion on a mandoline slicer, then use my handheld veg dicer to make them pleasingly dinky and even. I appreciate that that's a bit of work – although once adept at both of these gadgets it can be considerably faster than chopping them – so you can just dice them finely with a large, heavy sharp knife if you prefer.

Remove the sausages from the pan, leaving any residual fat behind, and set to one side for a moment. Add the veg. Reduce the heat to medium and cook for around 10 minutes, seasoning sparingly with salt but generously with pepper. Add the bacon, pop the sausages back in, and continue for another few minutes, until the veg is soft and the bacon cooked to your liking. Remove from the heat and set to one side.

Pop the kettle on to boil for the gravy, and measure the granules into a mug. Pour the boiling water over and stir well until the gravy thickens, then set to one side.

Now return to your corn-milk pan. Warm it through on a medium heat until it starts to simmer, but be careful not to let it boil as milk can be very temperamental when hot! Add the instant mash and cheese and stir briskly and continuously until it forms a smooth mash. It may be slightly loose at this point, but it will firm up as it cools slightly.

Serve the mash in the middle of the bowl, top with the veg-bacon mix, add a pair of sausages, and cover the lot generously with gravy. Serve piping hot and enjoy!

TO KEEP: Store in an airtight container, covered bowl or food storage bag in the fridge for up to 3 days. Reheat to piping hot to serve. The mash is suitable for freezing; the veg and bacon less so.

LEMON AND ROSEMARY ROAST POTATOES

This reminds me of my childhood and of funerals of Greek relatives, where these fragrant potatoes would be piled high on the buffet table. The language of grief in my family lineage is expressed in carbohydrates, and as a result these are one of the comfort-blanket recipes that I reach for when the British equivalent – hot sweet tea – doesn't quite cut it.

SERVES 6–8, DEPENDING ON APPETITE AND ACCOMPANIMENTS

2kg potatoes
a few generous
    pinches of salt
100g lard
100ml light cooking oil
2 tbsp plain flour
1 tbsp mixed dried herbs
plenty of black pepper
2 tbsp lemon juice

First, peel your potatoes and cut them into thirds or quarters, depending on their size. Keep the peel – you can use them in a soup or in the veg-peel falafels on page 82, or to make fishcakes with a tin of sardines, or add them to mash. Just don't throw them away!

Preheat the oven to 190°C/fan 170°C/375°F/gas 5.

Bring a huge saucepan, half-filled with cold fresh water, to a rolling boil. (A rolling boil is where large bubbles rise quickly to the surface of the water in the pan, often in a 'rolling' motion from the outside edges inwards, hence the name.) Add the potatoes carefully, salt the water generously and reduce the heat to medium to allow them to simmer. If you have a lid for the pan, pop it on to trap the heat and speed up the cooking time; if you don't, a sturdy plate or large frying pan popped over the top does the same job. Simmer for around 8 minutes.

While the potatoes are simmering, add your lard and oil to a roasting tin. Place it in the oven, at the bottom, to get hot. (If you place it too near the top the fat may burn!)

While the potatoes are simmering and the fat is sizzling, make your seasoned flour coating. Spoon the flour into a small bowl or mug, and add some salt, the herbs and plenty of black pepper. Mix well to distribute evenly and set to one side for a moment.

Drain the potatoes well and jostle them about a little to fluff up the edges. Sprinkle over the seasoned flour mixture and toss the potatoes gently to coat them lightly in it. Remove the hot fat pan from the oven and carefully place each potato into it – I like to pop them in a few at a time with a serving spoon, but if you stand well back and do it gently you may be brave enough to tip the lot into the sizzling fat. An avalanche of potatoes and a spitting pan of lard, however, are bedfellows to be particularly cautious around!

However your potatoes end up in the pan, ensure that they are in one single layer, and place them in the centre of the oven for 90 minutes, removing them to turn them over halfway through.

At the 'turning point', shake over some of your lemon juice and add a little more salt and pepper, before returning them to the oven.

Serve immediately, or reheat to piping hot to serve.

TO KEEP: Leftovers will keep in the fridge for up to 3 days, I'm afraid they've never been around long enough in my household for me to be able to advise how they would fare in the freezer!

PATATA, NTOMATA Ⓥ

This is a recipe for potato and herb dumplings in a classic Greek tomato sauce. In homage to my Greek-Cypriot roots, I decided to name this simple supper in Greek dialect. Naming a recipe is a complicated business; you want to convey the core elements, while also bringing in some of its purpose and personality. Too many words and you lose the surprises, or it becomes a prescriptive turnoff. Too few and you run the risk of loose interpretation. And that's the ballpark I play in, exuberantly, and unapologetically. My recipes are written as suggestives, rather than absolutes. For the sake of demonstrating this, I have left this one largely unedited – the 'word salad' below is the 70% that remains in my head when I commit recipes to paper. I hope it helps at least some of you feel a little more confident in your kitchens, whatever they may look like and wherever they may be. And the recipe title literally translates to Potato, Tomato, because at the end of the day, that's what I saw when I opened my fridge, that's what I grimaced at, wondering how I would make a meal of it, and those are the core ingredients. Everything else is just baubles.

SERVES 4

500g any kind of potatoes

a generous pinch of salt

150g plain flour, plus extra for dusting

1 egg

plenty of black pepper

1 large onion

4 fat cloves of garlic

2 tbsp light cooking oil

1 x 400g tin of plum or chopped tomatoes

1 tbsp vinegar or lemon juice

1 tbsp mixed dried herbs or 2 tbsp fresh ones

125ml water or stock

100g feta, Greek salad cheese or Cheddar

First wash and dice your spuds. You're not going to peel them, because firstly it's a laborious waste of time and secondly, a lot of the goodness and essential fibre is clinging to the underside of that skin there. And that needs to be in you, not in your trash. Not even in your compost heap. That's for you. And don't worry, you won't even be able to tell once it's all smashed up into lil' balls of gnocchi – well, it'll actually taste of something, but that's a good thing.

Pop them into a large saucepan that will easily hold twice their volume, and cover with cold water and then an extra two inches, to give them room for them to bob and jostle about when the bubbles kick in. Add a teaspoon of salt – you're going to drain it out again, it just helps aggravate the spuds to kick-start the softening process, and salt makes everything taste excellent.

Right, bring that pan to the boil, then reduce it to a simmer. Cover it with a lid – if you don't have a lid, improvise with a sturdy dinner plate, a baking tray, a bigger pan balanced on top, whatever, but you want to trap all that glorious heat in there because it'll make your spuds cook faster, conserve a little bit of energy, and when you take the lid off you basically get a starchy spa facial on top. Leave it alone for about 15 minutes – you want your spuds almost crumbling in the pan – then drain the water well and return the spuds to the pot. If you're organized you can drain the water into another pan and use it as the water and salt elements of your tomato sauce. The starch that's come out of the potatoes will help thicken your sauce as well, so you may need a little more than the 125ml quoted, but I'll trust you on that one.

Mash your potatoes – they'll need some vigorous work to loosen the skins, but once they're off, it's a pretty smooth operation from there. Stir in most of the flour – not all of it, as it'll get too stiff – then crack in the egg. Beat it in well with a fork to break it up and distribute it, then add the remaining flour. Season with plenty of black pepper, stir it all in and stand it to one side to cool for a moment – you don't want to be rolling something that's 70% freshly boiled water in your hands straight off the bat. So leave it alone, and get making your sauce while you wait.

Peel and finely slice or dice your onion, then peel the garlic and halve each clove lengthways. Heat the oil in a large non-stick pan and add the onion and garlic, season with a little salt and pepper and cook briefly on a high heat for 2–3 minutes to slightly soften.

Pour over your tin of tomatoes and all of the juice, then add your vinegar or lemon juice and herbs. Cook on a high heat for a couple more minutes, then add a splash of the reserved starchy potato water or stock and turn the heat down low.

Flour your hands so the potato mixture doesn't stick to them, and roll it into balls the size of a walnut in its shell. Pop each ball into the pan of sauce, jostling them every now and then to keep them separated. Add a splash more water or stock as required to keep the sauce loose. When the potato dumplings are all bobbing around in the saucepan, pop a lid on and simmer it all for around 10 minutes, until the dumplings are cooked through.

Add the cheese; crumbled if using feta or Greek salad cheese, coarsely grated if using Cheddar, and stir gently to melt it in. Season to taste with a little more pepper and serve.

TO KEEP: Store in an airtight container, covered bowl or food storage bag in the fridge for up to 3 days. Make sure the dumplings are well covered in sauce so they don't dry out. Reheat to piping hot to serve. Not recommended for freezing.

AN EXTRA HELPING

Dumplings, although no longer particularly fashionable, aren't exactly groundbreaking. Well, apart from the first ever ones I made, in a lamb stew for the man who is now the wonderful father to my son. They literally could have been used in close-contact warfare to maim or at least stun an encroaching opponent. I've practised since then, and now my dumplings sit on top of my soups and stews, not sunk like large drainage pebbles to the bottom of them.

I include this 'nugget' because I think it's important to be honest and authentic, and admit that learning to cook takes time, and disasters, and stoic munching your way through barely edible nonsense to set a good example to the kids. They're all rites of passage. Like your first burn. Your first small fire. Your first smashed dish full of dinner on the kitchen floor. Your first utterly destroyed pan. We all go through it, and the important thing to remember is to go through it, not sit there in that moment, telling yourself that it's useless trying to learn, or giving up. Just pick that casserole dish up, clean up and carry on. And if in doubt, always consult Delia Smith and cross reference her with Nigella Lawson.

EASY POTATO AND EGG CURRY ⓥ

This quick and easy dinner is always a hit with friends; it takes almost no effort to throw together and the end result is impressively delicious. Stretch it further by adding a tin of chickpeas or black beans, or cooked brown or green lentils – but if you do this, you may wish to add some more tomatoes and spices, as the pulses temper the overall flavour somewhat.

SERVES 2–4, DEPENDING ON APPETITES

4 eggs
1 large onion
1 tbsp light cooking oil
2 tbsp medium curry powder
a pinch of chilli powder
1 x 540g tin of potatoes
1 x 400g tin of chopped tomatoes
120g frozen or fresh spinach or kale
salt (optional)
120g natural yoghurt

TIP: *If boiling the eggs seems like hard work, you can just crack them in to poach at the end. It feels a little obscene, but it is rather tasty!*

Half-fill a medium saucepan with water and gently drop in the eggs. Bring it to the boil, then reduce to a simmer for around 6 minutes. Remove from the heat but leave them in the hot water to continue to hard-boil without using too much energy.

Meanwhile, peel and finely slice your onion. Heat the oil in a large frying pan and add the onion, then the curry powder and chilli powder. Cook over a medium heat for 5–6 minutes until the onion starts to soften.

Drain the potatoes – reserving the water to use in a moment – and slice them, then add them to the pan. They will likely spit when introduced to the hot oil, so be careful! Stir them into the onions and curry powder to gently coat them, then fry for a further 3–4 minutes. All you're doing at this stage is crisping the edges a little.

Gently remove the eggs from the hot water and carefully place them in a small bowl. Cover them with fresh cold water – to prevent them cooking any further.

Pour over the chopped tomatoes, add the spinach, and stir well. Bring to the boil very briefly, then reduce to a simmer for around 15 minutes. If it starts to dry out, add the reserved water from the potato tin; it will be slightly salty and starchy, so I haven't added any extra salt to this recipe, but you can adjust it to taste if you like.

While the curry is simmering, remove your eggs from the cold water and peel them gently. Discard the shells (they are excellent slug deterrents in the garden). Halve the eggs lengthways and nestle into the hot curry for a minute to warm through.

Remove from the heat, stir in the yoghurt, and serve immediately.

TO KEEP: Leftovers will keep for 2 days in the fridge. If you eat all of the eggs but still have some potato curry left, you can freeze this for up to 3 months, but heat it through gently to serve, or else the yoghurt may split.

KOLOKITHOKEFTEDES Ⓥ

The inclusion of instant mashed potato powder in this recipe is absolutely illegitimate, but it does impart a deliciously soft and fluffy texture and help absorb any excess liquid from the courgettes, resulting in a crispier bite. I have every confidence that if I were hauled before my Aunty Helen Constantine and Grandad John Savvas Hadjicostas at the Pearly Gates to explain myself, I'd be able to make a convincing case for its inclusion. And to be honest, if I could get it past them, it's pretty much an almost acceptable level of culinary deviance. Almost . . .

SERVES 4 AS A MEZZE, STARTER OR SNACK

1 large courgette
1 tsp salt
some patience
1 medium onion
2 tsp mixed dried herbs
2 tbsp instant mashed potato flakes
1 tbsp flour, plus extra for dusting
plenty of black pepper
oil, for frying

For the dipping sauce
200ml natural yoghurt
1 tbsp sunflower oil
1 small clove of garlic
a fistful of chopped fresh basil, parsley or mint, or 1 more tsp mixed dried herbs
a pinch of black pepper
1 tsp lemon juice

Coarsely grate your courgette into a bowl, add the salt, and mix well to distribute it throughout. Transfer to a fine-mesh sieve and balance this over a pan or mixing bowl to catch the excess liquid as it drains. Leave to stand for at least 20 minutes for the salt to draw the moisture from the courgette, stirring a couple of times to help it along the way.

Meanwhile, make the dipping sauce. Measure the yoghurt into a mug or small bowl, and add the oil. Peel and finely grate or mince the garlic, and add along with the herbs and pepper. Mix well to combine and set to one side.

Peel and finely slice your onion and pop it into a large mixing bowl, along with the mixed dried herbs. When your courgettes are done, gently squeeze them in your hands to drain as much of the remaining salty liquid as possible, then add to the onions and mix well. Spoon in the potato, flour and the black pepper, then mix everything together until it starts to stick. If it is slightly too dry, add a tablespoon of the reserved courgette liquid and mix again. If it's a little too wet, add an extra tablespoon of mash.

Heat the oil in a large non-stick pan and flour your hands so the mixture doesn't stick to them too much. Shape it into walnut-sized balls and place them carefully into the hot oil, flattening them slightly with a fork as you do. Fry for a few minutes on each side until crisp and golden, then remove from the heat. You may need to cook these in batches, depending on how deft you are and how large your pan is.

Stir the lemon juice into the yoghurt just before serving, and enjoy hot or cold. Delicious warmed through or just eaten cold as they come.

TO KEEP: Will keep in the fridge for up to 3 days.

Leabharlanna Fhine Gall

PASTA, RICE AND OTHER GRAINS

Quick, cheerful, filling and endlessly customizable, pasta and rice are the things we eat most often in my household.

For pasta, the cheapest varieties at the supermarket tend to be spaghetti and penne, and both are versatile enough that you don't really need any others, but being something of a glutton for starchy carbs, and something of an avid collector of all kinds of nonsense, I'll admit that I have quite the collection of varied pasta shapes myself. I'm almost obligated to recommend that if you can afford the few pence extra for wholegrain pasta, do invest in a bag once in a while, but don't make the mistake I did of mixing the wholegrain with the white stuff in the same jar because they cook at different rates, leaving you with some soggy pieces and some that are rather too al dente in the same dinner. Many an evening meal begins with me asking my son: 'What pasta shape do you want for dinner tonight?' And even after almost a decade of writing recipes, the response will come back: 'Twisty ones!' 'You mean fusilli. . .' 'Little bows!' 'Farfalle. . .' and so on, and so forth.

Although brown rice is arguably better for you than white, it's not so great for your wallet, unfortunately! I use cheap white long grain rice for everything — even risotto — and it works just fine. Yes, arborio rice is better, but again, it's around six times the price of the value rice, and I'd rather have six dinners that are absolutely fine than one that is only marginally better. All of the recipes in this chapter can be made with plain white, long grain rice, but if you fancy experimenting a little, pearl barley is an inexpensive, nutty-tasting, stubby little grain that will work as a substitute in any of the following dishes. I flick between the two over the next few pages, to keep it interesting, but you can use one or the other as you prefer.

TOMATO, BREAD AND BUTTER PASTA ⓥ

A really simple dish that can make use of discarded ends of bread or crusts of sandwiches and turns them into something unrecognizably delicious. You can use this as a base and add anything you fancy to it; some cooked frozen peppers, olives, tinned fish, frozen spinach – whatever takes your fancy!

SERVES 4

6 cloves of garlic

1 stock cube

70g baking block or butter, or 3 tbsp light cooking oil

2 slices of bread

2 x 400g tins of plum or chopped tomatoes

a small handful of fresh basil, mint, parsley or coriander, or 2 tsp dried herbs

1 tbsp light-coloured vinegar

300ml boiling water or stock

250g spaghetti

plenty of black pepper

First grate your garlic into a large pan, but don't place it on the heat just yet as garlic is fragile and burns easily. Crush your stock cube and sprinkle it over to season the garlic thoroughly, then add the butter. Place the pan on the smallest hob ring on a low heat, stirring for a minute or two as the butter starts to melt and the garlic gently, gently sizzles.

Dice the bread into 2.5cm squares, or thereabouts, and toss into the pan. Pour over your tomatoes and mash roughly with the side of a wooden spoon or spatula to break them up a little. Add your herbs and a splash of vinegar. Simmer for 25 minutes, stirring occasionally and topping up with the boiling water or stock as required – you want a thick and textured sauce, but still loose enough to be comfortingly sloppy. How much liquid you'll need will depend on the type and age of bread used, and your personal preference.

When the sauce is 10 minutes from being finished, bring a pan of water to the boil and salt it generously. Add your pasta and reduce the heat to a simmer. Cover with a lid, or if you don't have a lid a large sturdy dinner plate or baking tray will do, and simmer for 8 minutes or until tender. Strain the pasta, toss with the sauce and serve immediately.

TO KEEP: Leftovers will keep in the fridge for up to 3 days, or in the freezer for up to 3 months.

SALMON, LEMON, PEA AND SWEETCORN PASTA

A simple jar of fish paste is the star of the show here, and it really works for a creamy pasta sauce. I first made a version of this in my first cookbook, *A Girl Called Jack*, and it remains one of the most popular recipes on my website. I've given it a little upgrade here with some colourful veggies for a bit of extra goodness. If salmon paste isn't to your liking, or you don't have any in your local shop, tuna paste works just as well.

SERVES 4

plenty of salt
300g spaghetti
200g frozen peas
200g frozen sweetcorn
150g salmon paste
60ml milk
1 tbsp lemon juice
plenty of black pepper

Generously salt a medium saucepan of water. Bring it to the boil, then add all of the pasta. Reduce the heat to a simmer and allow to cook for 8–10 minutes. Add the peas and sweetcorn halfway through to defrost and cook so that they're lovely and tender.

While the pasta and peas cook, grab a small bowl and beat together the salmon paste, milk and lemon juice. I find that using a fork helps to break up the salmon paste and combine it to a smooth sauce, as some of the cheaper jars can be a bit grainy or thick. Add a tablespoon or two of the hot salty pasta water to soften it and give it a headstart if needed, and season generously with black pepper.

When the pasta is cooked, remove from the heat and drain well. Tip the pasta and veg back into the pan, and pour over the sauce, stirring to coat, then serve.

TO KEEP: It will keep in the fridge for up to 3 days. If you want to freeze it, I recommend adding a tin of coconut milk or tomatoes to the sauce to make it wetter, otherwise you run the risk of 'freezer burn' or slightly dry pasta.

BLACK AND CHEESE

This recipe is incredibly popular with my friends and family – even lifelong black-pudding refuseniks have been converted by its simple, cheesy and comforting deliciousness. Black pudding is cheap and nutritious, although if it's not to your liking, feel free to substitute with any sausage you'd prefer.

SERVES 4

3 tbsp baking spread or butter

3 tbsp flour

1 tsp English mustard

600ml milk

200g mature or medium Cheddar cheese, grated

250g macaroni or penne pasta

salt and black pepper

230g black pudding

1 tbsp cooking oil

1 slice of bread, grated or blitzed into breadcrumbs

First melt the baking spread or butter in a small pan and stir in the flour evenly to make a roux. Spoon in the mustard, then gradually add the milk, whisking it in a little bit at a time. Add three-quarters of the cheese and continue to cook the sauce for around 10 minutes, until it thickens substantially and the cheese has melted. Remove it from the heat and stand it to one side while everything else comes together.

Bring a pan of water to the boil and salt it generously. Add your pasta and reduce to a simmer, then cover. Simmer according to the packet instructions – usually around 6 minutes until just al dente. Preheat the oven to 190°C/ fan 170°C/375°F/gas 5.

While the pasta is cooking, dice your black pudding into 1cm pieces. Heat the cooking oil in a large non-stick pan and add the pudding pieces. Fry for around 6–8 minutes, jostling every now and then to ensure all the sides get a bit crispy.

All three elements should come together at around the same time, but if that's not the case for you, don't fret about it! Strain the pasta and transfer it to a 22cm baking dish, then evenly scatter over the black pudding and pour over the sauce. Top with the breadcrumbs and remaining cheese, and plenty of black pepper. Bake in the centre of the oven for around 20 minutes, or until golden and bubbling. Allow to cool for a few minutes before serving.

TO KEEP: Allow to cool completely, then store in the fridge in an airtight container, covered bowl or food storage bag, and enjoy within 3 days. Can be eaten hot or cold – both are delicious! It will keep in the freezer for up to 3 months; defrost completely and reheat to piping hot throughout to serve.

SNEAKY VEG AND LENTIL BOLOGNESE

Padding out Bolognese sauce with finely chopped vegetables and lentils makes the meat go much further – and also adds extra vitamins and nutrients. You can use almost any vegetable you like in this, although anything from the brassica family might impart a slightly bitter undertone, so use those sparingly. If you're cooking for vegan or vegetarian palates, simply omit the mince and replace with either soya mince or your favourite veggie equivalent. Finely chopped or coarsely grated mushrooms work well as a vegetarian or vegan mince replacement, too!

MAKES 8 PORTIONS

240g dried green or brown lentils

2 large onions or 3 medium ones

2 large carrots

4 generous celery stalks

12 decent-sized mushrooms

1 tbsp cooking oil

300g beef mince

2 tsp mixed dried herbs

800g tinned chopped tomatoes

1 tbsp light-coloured vinegar

2 tbsp tomato ketchup

1 tbsp gravy granules

salt and black pepper

First pop the lentils into a bowl of cold water to soak for around 8 hours. Drain and rinse very thoroughly, then pop them into a pan of fresh, cold, unsalted water that will easily hold thrice their volume. Bring to the boil, then reduce to a simmer on the back of the stove, tucked out of the way, for around 20 minutes.

Peel and very finely chop your onions, and finely chop your carrots, celery and mushrooms. If you have a food processor, sling them all in and pulse a few times. If you don't, you can chop them finely with a large, heavy sharp knife, or grate it all using the large holes on a standard box grater. However you achieve it, you want them all in an even, mince-like texture.

Warm the oil in a large, non-stick pan and add your veg. Break up the mince and add that too, then fry for 4–5 minutes on a high heat to start to soften the veg and seal the mince. Add the herbs, chopped tomatoes, vinegar, ketchup and gravy granules. Pour over 250ml of cold water and bring to the boil. Reduce to a simmer and stir occasionally to prevent it from sticking to the bottom of the pan.

When the lentils are soft and swollen, drain them thoroughly and rinse well under cold running water, then add to the sauce. Stir, and pour over another 200ml of water, then bring back to the boil and reduce to a simmer. Salt generously, season with plenty of black pepper and simmer for a further 15 minutes.

Serve with your choice of pasta – controversially, I like Bolognese with conchiglie, as the shells are a perfect vessel for little piles of chunky sauce, but spaghetti, penne, fusilli and bucatini all work well too.

TO KEEP: Leftover sauce will keep in the fridge for up to 3 days, or can be frozen for up to 3 months.

MUSHROOM AND BLUE CHEESE PASTA ⓥ

This pasta sauce works best with a spaghetti or other long pasta, but conchiglie shells or other small pasta would also be delicious, like little boats of sloppy salty creamy goodness. Oh my. I used frozen diced onion in the first iteration of this dish, because I am all about saving precious minutes and streaky mascara wherever possible, but fresh onions work just fine too.

SERVES 2

160g white onion
2 tbsp oil or butter
salt and black pepper
300g mushrooms
1 tbsp plain flour
300ml milk
100g blue cheese –
   I used Stilton
a pinch of mixed
   dried herbs or
   rosemary or thyme
140g penne or spaghetti

First peel and dice your onion, then toss it into a large, non-stick pan with 1 tablespoon of the oil or butter, and a little salt and pepper. Cook on a very low heat on the smallest burner for 8–10 minutes until starting to soften. Finely slice your mushrooms and add those too, and cook for 4–5 minutes more, until they start to colour.

Remove the onion and mushrooms with a slotted spoon, leaving any juices in the pan, and place them in the large cup of a small bullet blender. (If you don't have a bullet blender, don't worry, you can leave them in whole, but serve with chunky pasta instead for best results.)

Add another tablespoon of oil to the pan, still on a low heat, and quickly stir in the flour to make a rough paste. Thin with 2 tablespoons of milk, beating swiftly and firmly, and repeat until half of the milk is incorporated. Crumble in the cheese and add the rest of the milk, then turn the heat up to medium to melt the cheese and thicken the sauce.

Pour the cheese sauce over the mushrooms and onion in the blender, and blend until smooth. Return to the pan. Stir in the herbs and some more black pepper. Leave to cool and thicken off the heat.

Bring a separate pan of water to the boil, salt it generously and pour in the pasta. Reduce to a simmer and cover if you have a lid for it (a dinner plate or larger pan will do at a pinch). Simmer for 8–10 minutes until the pasta is soft, stirring once or twice to prevent it from sticking and burning at the bottom of the pan.

Drain the pasta and tip into the mushroom and blue cheese sauce, stirring to coat. Bring back to the heat and warm through to serve.

TO KEEP: Leftover sauce will keep in the fridge for up to 3 days in a covered bowl, airtight container or food storage bag, or can be frozen for up to 3 months.

TOMATO, CHILLI AND CRAB PASTA SAUCE

This recipe is an absolute riff on a Gordon Ramsay dish that I cooked one Valentine's Day night, in a long-ago life, well before I ever did this for a living. I dutifully wrote the original down in a little black notebook and found it again a decade later when emptying boxes from yet another house move. It was fascinating to see how my cooking had changed as my circumstances had, and I set about reworking the 'old life' recipes to be suitable for this one. Out went the king prawns, in came the crab paste. Out went the fresh egg linguine and in came the budget dried spaghetti – and so on and so forth. The result is still utterly delicious, if slightly less of a seductive showstopper. But as a bonus point, no messy fingers with crab paste and no eyes to contend with either. (Eye-ther?)

SERVES 2

2 tbsp light cooking oil
1 large onion
salt and black pepper
a pinch of dried chilli flakes
1 x 75g jar of crab paste
400g passata or tinned
  chopped tomatoes
1 tbsp lemon juice
a handful of fresh
  basil or parsley
150g spaghetti

Heat the oil in a large non-stick pan. Peel and finely slice your onion and add to the pan. Season generously with salt and pepper and add your chilli flakes. Fry on a low heat for 10 minutes to start to soften, stirring occasionally to disturb the onion so it doesn't catch and burn on the bottom of the pan.

Spoon the crab paste into a mug or small jug and add an equal quantity of passata or chopped tomatoes to it. Add the lemon juice and mix briskly and well with a fork to loosen the crab paste to a smoother, pourable consistency. Pour this over the onion and add the remaining passata or tomatoes. Finely chop the herbs, including any soft stalks, and add three-quarters too. Cook on a medium heat for around 20 minutes, stirring intermittently, until the sauce is thick and glossy. Taste and add more pepper, lemon or chilli, if you like. Serve over cooked spaghetti or pasta with the reserved herbs to garnish.

TO KEEP: Leftover sauce will keep in the fridge for up to 3 days, or can be frozen for up to 3 months. If you have leftover spaghetti as well, combine with the sauce with a splash of water to loosen it, ensuring all of the spaghetti is coated to prevent it from drying out, then store in an airtight container or freezer bag in the fridge for up to 2 days. Can be enjoyed warm or cold, as takes your fancy.

RATATOUILLE Ⓥⓔ

The first time I made this, I served it atop a jacket potato and I was absolutely, utterly delighted with it. So delighted, in fact, I made it twice in the same week, just for the sheer joy of it, and to assuage my guilt that it had taken me so long to finally give in to what is, by all accounts, a reasonably easy recipe. To make this even simpler, you can use frozen onions and peppers, both of which work absolutely fine. These days I like to serve it on top of a pile of hot pasta, but rice, mash, bread or any kind of carb will do.

And I feel obliged to add that the price of aubergines seems to have fluctuated wildly over the last few years; sometimes they seem perfectly reasonable as part of a modest weekly shop, and at other times I simply can't justify them, so if you happen to find yourself in the pricing silly season, simply replace the aubergine with an extra courgette, which tend to be far cheaper all year round. *(Pictured on the next page)*

SERVES 4

2 large onions

8 fat cloves of garlic

1 fresh pepper, any colour, or 120g frozen sliced peppers

2 tbsp light cooking oil

salt and black pepper

1 large aubergine

2 medium courgettes

800g tinned chopped tomatoes

2 tsp light-coloured vinegar

a pinch of sugar or your sweetener of choice

2 tsp mixed dried herbs, or a fistful of fresh ones (see opposite)

200g penne

First peel and finely slice your onions, and toss into a large non-stick pan. Peel your garlic cloves and quarter them lengthways, then add to the pan. Slice the pepper, discarding any clumps of seeds – I'm not too meticulous about this to be honest, but some people prefer not to have them in, so do what you feel is best. Measure in the oil, season with a little salt and pepper, and set the pan over a low heat. Cook for 5 minutes, stirring gently, to start to soften.

Dice your aubergine and courgettes and add to the pan, then quickly pour over the chopped tomatoes to stop them from browning as they are exposed to the air. Aubergines turn very quickly once chopped; they're fine to use once they start to discolour, they just don't look brilliant. Add the vinegar, sugar and herbs, and turn up the heat.

Cook on a medium heat, stirring, for 30 minutes, until the veg is soft but not mushy, and the liquid reduced, thickened and glossy. Season with a little extra salt and pepper to taste.

Towards the end of the cooking time, bring a pan of water to boil and salt it generously. Add your dried pasta and simmer for 8–10 minutes, or according to the packet instructions. When the pasta is cooked, drain it and toss with the ratatouille to serve.

TO KEEP: Can be served hot or cold; this is one of those dishes that improves with a rest and a reheat, so it will keep well in the fridge for 2 days, or if cooled completely, the ratatouille can be frozen for up to 3 months.

AN EXTRA HELPING

Ratatouille is one of those recipes that I, being entirely self-taught, had a strange fear about attempting to cook. My knowledge of it stemmed entirely from a Pixar movie starring an excitable animated rat. Even the name alone felt precise and intimidating.

And then one day a couple of years ago, the triumvirate of courgette, aubergine and pepper whispering from the fridge, I decided to give it a go. I dug out some of my French cookery books – *French Provincial Cooking* by Elizabeth David, *The Little Paris Kitchen* by Rachel Khoo and Elisabeth Luard's *Classic French Cooking* – all liberated from various secondhand stores over the years, added Sarah Raven's *Garden Cookbook* and set to work. This is how I work when trying something new; I compare and contrast three or four recipes, picking out the fundamentals and common denominators, then weave in what I think will be the best bits from each, to my own tastes and intuition. Most of the time, it works a charm.

The four cookery writers above all differ wildly on the use of herbs – Luard uses rosemary and thyme, David has coriander seeds, basil and parsley, Raven uses fresh coriander, and Khoo uses thyme, so I have opted for mixed dried herbs – a blend of thyme, marjoram, oregano, parsley, sage and basil – the best of all of them, with a few little extras, just because.

Some of the classic recipes insist on 2 cups of oil, and my constitution just wouldn't tolerate that at all, never mind my wallet, so I have used a far more modest amount.

PASTITSIO (GREEK LASAGNE)

Pastitsio is a food that reminds me of my childhood; snaffled from piled-high buffet plates at various relatives' houses following Greek Orthodox church services – usually a christening or a funeral. My aunties would make them; huge trays of something that was a cross between a lasagne and a macaroni cheese, and it is the ultimate cut-and-come-again comfort food. Delicious hot, cold or lukewarm at any time of day. *(Pictured on previous page)*

SERVES 6–8

For the bechamel

60ml cooking oil

50g flour

400ml milk

scant ½ tsp mustard – any kind

100g mozzarella, grated, plus extra (optional)

a pinch of ground nutmeg

salt and black pepper

For the mince

1 onion

2 large celery stalks

4 fat cloves of garlic or 6 dinky ones

1 medium carrot

2 tbsp cooking oil

½ tsp ground cinnamon

1 tsp mixed dried herbs

a pinch of powdered clove or 2 whole cloves

salt and black pepper

500g mince – pork is traditional, but any will do

175ml strong black tea or red wine if you have it

500g passata or 1 x 400g tin of chopped tomatoes plus 100ml water

First prepare the mince. Peel and very finely chop your onion, and finely slice the celery and garlic cloves. Grate your carrot, including the peel and the top, using the large holes on a box grater. Heat 2 tablespoons of oil on your largest hob ring in a very large non-stick pan, and add the veg. Turn the heat down to low – the large hob will still give off a generous amount of firepower – and add the cinnamon, herbs and cloves. Season generously with salt and pepper, and cook gently for around 10 minutes, keeping the veg moving every now and then so they don't stick and burn.

Add your mince and stir it through the veg, until lightly browned. Pour over the tea or wine, passata and stock. Stir in the vinegar and sugar. Bring to the boil, briefly, then reduce to a simmer, uncovered, for around 20 minutes.

While the mince is cooking, make your bechamel. To do this, add the oil to a small pan over a medium heat and stir in the flour to form a 'roux' (a kind of paste). Gradually pour in the milk a little at a time, whisking after each addition until the sauce is smooth and you've used all the milk. Reduce the heat to low and allow to simmer, stirring regularly until the sauce is smooth and thick. Stir in the mustard, mozzarella, nutmeg, and salt and pepper.

Bring a large, wide pan of generously salted water to the boil, and add the pasta. Slightly undercook it so it is al dente, as it will continue to cook in the oven – around 6–7 minutes is fine for most dried pastas, but check the packet instructions and simply knock 1–2 minutes off the cooking time. When the pasta goes into the pot, turn your oven on to 180°C/fan 160°C/350°F/gas 4 and lightly grease your baking dish (roughly 22 x 30cm).

Drain the pasta and return it to the pan. Add a ladle of the bechamel and shake the pan gently to lightly coat the pasta.

125ml strong mushroom
or vegetable stock
or weak gravy (see
pages 218 and 222
for homemade)

1 tsp light-coloured
vinegar

1 tbsp sugar

plus 300g tubular
pasta – bucatini is
traditional but penne
and macaroni are fine

Transfer half of the pasta to the bottom of the baking dish. If you want to be fastidious about it, you can try to make sure the pasta is all aligned neatly so when it is cut through it looks spectacularly neat and really quite awesome, but Greek and Cypriot cooking is more of a practical skill than a beauty pageant, so you can just pop it in however you like.

Stir a ladle of bechamel into the mince and sauce, then spread it evenly over the pasta. Layer the remaining pasta on top, then pour over the remaining bechamel. You can top this with extra cheese if you like, but it's not essential.

Bake in the centre of the oven for 30 minutes, then remove and allow to cool to room temperature before enjoying.

TO KEEP: Can be stored in the fridge for 3 days, or in the freezer for up to 6 months. Delicious enjoyed fridge-cold, at room temperature (as is traditional) or piping hot.

TIP: If you have a small bullet blender, making the bechamel sauce is even easier. Weigh the flour into the largest cup for the blender, and add the oil, mustard, mozzarella, a pinch of nutmeg, salt and pepper and two-thirds of the milk. Blend for 60 seconds, or until smooth. It will look a little thin, but it thickens up when warmed, just like in the traditional method. Transfer it into a saucepan, on a low heat on your smallest hob ring, and stir intermittently to keep it smooth, adding the remaining milk a little at a time. When it has thickened sufficiently that it thickly coats the back of your wooden spoon, remove from the heat. It will continue to firm up – don't be alarmed by this – but if it starts to set, loosen it with a little of the boiling pasta water from the next step.

CHICKPEA, CHARD AND LEMON PASTA Ⓥⓔ

I grow chard at home; it's one of the few plants that I manage to actually keep alive, and I'm on my third year from the same single (benignly neglected) packet of seeds, so if you have a sunny window ledge, balcony or small outdoor space, I can highly recommend it as effortless and bountiful. If you don't have any chard to hand, you can use spring greens, green cabbage, spinach or kale instead. This recipe is extremely simple and very filling – the cumin and paprika flavours make it warming and hearty enough for cold autumn and winter evenings, whereas the fresh greens and lemon bring it into a light summer lunch – so it's a year-round versatile staple. I have left this recipe deliberately very simple, but you can add more vegetables to it if you have them to hand. Use this recipe as a baseline and adapt it to hoover up all manner of odds and sods in your fridge – diced root vegetables work well, as do finely sliced mushrooms, aubergine or courgette. Make it go further by cracking one egg per person into the top a few minutes before serving, or by adding some torn fresh or stale bread – or crusts – to thicken it.

SERVES 4

1 large onion

2 tbsp light cooking oil

a generous pinch of salt

4 fat cloves of garlic

1 tbsp cumin, seeds or ground

1 tsp smoked paprika or 2 tsp sweet

1 x 400g tin of chickpeas

1 x 400g tin of plum or chopped tomatoes

1 vegetable stock cube

140g small pasta, such as orzo, or broken-up spaghetti

a few handfuls of fresh chard or spring greens, or frozen spinach or kale

lemon juice and plenty of black pepper, to taste

First peel and dice your onion, nice and small. Warm the oil in a large non-stick pan on a medium heat and add the onion. Season with a pinch of salt and cook for 8–10 minutes, stirring every now and then to disturb them so they don't catch on the bottom of the pan.

Peel your garlic cloves and halve them lengthways, then roughly chop and add to the pan, along with the cumin and paprika. Stir everything together, and cook for just a minute more, before adding the whole tin of chickpeas, including the liquid. Pour over the tomatoes and add the stock cube. Bring briefly to the boil – but not for more than a moment – then reduce to a low simmer. Cover and simmer for 45 minutes, until the chickpeas are very soft and the soup has thickened.

Stir the pasta in, cover and simmer for 12–15 minutes (see Tip).

When the pasta is cooked, finely chop your chard, if using, or drop in your frozen spinach or other greens. Fresh chard will take under a minute to cook; frozen blocks of spinach can take up to 4 or 5.

Dress with lemon juice to taste and plenty of black pepper, and serve.

TO KEEP: This dish can be made in advance and reheated as required. It will keep well in the fridge in an airtight bag or container for up to 4 days, or up to 3 months in the freezer.

TIP: Cooking pasta in a liquid base other than water tends to take longer than the packet instructions advise; I've found anything from 1.5 times the stated time to double it is about right for tomato-based sauces and stews, but you may like your pasta more or less al dente than mine, so keep an eye on it and nibble a bit here and there to find your bite point.

CHICKENESTRONE
(LA ZUPPA DI UNO SCIOCCO)

This recipe is a favourite for convalescence in my small household; ideal 'bowl food', to be slowly supped and savoured from a favourite corner of the couch, or as a very rare treat, propped up on pillows in bed if one is recovering from a stomach ache or other minor malady. It can be easily made vegan or vegetarian by swapping the stock cube for an equivalent; Osem powdered stock is both vegan and kosher as well as convincingly flavoured, or a reasonable-quality vegetable bouillon powder will do the same job. As you may have guessed from the liberty I've taken with the name, this is a portmanteau between the classic Italian minestrone soup, and a chicken one. I did consult with an Italian friend before smashing the two together in the public domain and she laughed, and affectionately nicknamed it 'la zuppa di uno sciocco – the soup of a fool'.

SERVES 2

1 large onion
2 celery stalks (optional)
1 medium carrot
4 fat cloves of garlic
1 tbsp light cooking oil
a generous pinch of salt
1 x 400g tin of cannellini, borlotti or pinto beans
2 chicken stock cubes
1 tsp mixed dried herbs
plenty of black pepper
60g spaghetti
a handful of greens: spring greens, kale, spinach, green cabbage or mixed salad leaves all work
2 tsp lemon juice

Peel and finely slice your onion and slice the celery, if using. Wash and finely slice your carrot. Peel the garlic and quarter the cloves lengthways.

Heat the oil in a large non-stick pan and add the veg, then season with a pinch of salt. Cook on a medium–high heat for 4–5 minutes, stirring occasionally to disturb them, so they start to slightly soften.

Open your tin of beans and add to the pot, along with all of the liquid from the tin. Crumble in the stock cubes and add the herbs and plenty of black pepper. Refill the empty bean tin with cold tap water and add half of this to the pan, keeping the other half in case you need it in a moment. Simmer everything together for around 15 minutes.

Break your spaghetti into 2cm pieces and add these to the pot, then simmer for 10–12 minutes more. The spaghetti will take slightly longer than usual to cook due to the viscosity of the cooking liquid being trickier to absorb than plain salted water would be.

When the soup is cooked, finely chop your greens and toss them in for half a minute to wilt, then add the lemon juice and a little more pepper to serve.

TO KEEP: This will keep in the fridge for up to 3 days, or in the freezer for 3 months. Defrost thoroughly in the fridge overnight or at room temperature for 4–6 hours, and reheat to piping hot to serve.

RISOTTO WITH PEAS AND LETTUCE

The suggestion to put cold lettuce leaves into a warm dish may seem unusual, but it is one of my favourite things. It is definitely not a revolutionary idea; gently wilted lettuce has topped slick hot burgers for a hundred years or thereabouts, so there must be something in it. If the idea really makes you shudder, use a hardier leaf for this recipe, like spinach, chard or cabbage, but I promise you, this is truly delightful.

SERVES 4

300g rice
1 tbsp oil or baking spread
2 stock cubes dissolved in 750ml boiling water or 750ml chicken or vegetable stock (see page 218 for homemade)
2 tbsp lemon juice
200g frozen peas
a pinch of pepper
¼ head of lettuce

TIP: *I find it is perfectly delicious without, but you could add 2 tbsp white wine in with the first tablespoon of lemon juice if you like.*

Grab a wide, shallow-based non-stick saucepan and pop it on the hob. Shake in your rice and add the oil or baking spread, then turn up the heat to gently toast it at the edges for a minute or two.

Add a splash of stock, and stir well to stop the rice from sticking and burning. Add a splash more. When it has been absorbed, add a splash more, and repeat until two-thirds of the stock has been used. This may seem laborious, but to me it is one of the joys of making a risotto; the ability to stand still for 20 minutes and lose myself in the methodical stirring and rhythmic hypnosis of a repetitive, gentle task. When the rice is starting to swell and almost all of the stock is absorbed, splash in the rest, along with 1 tablespoon of lemon juice.

Add the peas and pepper, and stir well. Finely slice the lettuce and set to one side; you will fold this through (gently stir it in) right at the very end, as do it any earlier and you will end up with a soggy rotten mess!

When the risotto is finished – that is, the rice is soft and sitting in a sticky, creamy liquid, bejewelled with bright green peas – remove it from the heat. Gently fold in the lettuce to wilt it, dash over the rest of the lemon juice and an extra smattering of pepper, and serve immediately for best results.

TO KEEP: Leftovers will keep in the fridge for up to 3 days, but because of the rice content must be cooled completely before refrigerating and then be reheated until piping hot. This can also be frozen for up to 3 months, then defrosted and heated until piping hot.

PEARL BARLEY AVGOLEMONO

Avgolemono is one of my most favourite comfort foods; regular readers will have seen it in varying iterations by now, but for the uninitiated it's a Greek egg and lemon soup that's reminiscent of my childhood, as Mum would always have a pot of it on the back of the stove after the Sunday roast. It seemed to have magical properties – filling, nourishing, the culinary equivalent of a maternal hug or a heavy duvet on a cold night. Although it's traditionally made with rice, this version uses pearl barley for a change, but if you don't have any pearl barley you can swap it for rice without changing the method at all. You can add some finely chopped greens if you have them kicking around; spring greens, chard, collard greens, kale and spinach all work well, as does a fistful of finely chopped parsley, stalks and all.

MAKES 2 GENEROUS BOWLS

100g pearl barley

600ml chicken or vegetable stock (see page 218 for homemade)

2 medium eggs

2 tbsp lemon juice, plus extra to serve

plenty of black pepper, to serve

Measure your pearl barley into a large saucepan and add all of the stock. Bring it to the boil, then reduce to a simmer. Cover, and simmer for around 40 minutes.

When the pearl barley is very soft, remove the pan from the heat and set to one side.

Crack the eggs into a mug or small bowl and add the lemon juice. Beat well with a fork to completely combine.

Carefully transfer a tablespoon of the hot stock from the pan to the mug with the egg and lemon mixture in. Beat well, then add another, combining completely before adding the next one. Do not rush this step, it is important that the eggs come to a warmer temperature gradually, else they will scramble, and that's not what we're going for at all here.

When the mug is almost full, pour the contents slowly back into the saucepan and stir in briskly.

Serve immediately, with extra lemon juice and plenty of black pepper.

TO KEEP: Will keep in the fridge for 2 days; make sure it is completely cool before chilling, and reheat until piping hot throughout to serve. Not recommended for freezing because of the egg–lemon base – it goes a bit weird in the freezer!

MUSHROOM AND LENTIL BARLOTTO Ⓥ

I used to be quite intimidated by pearl barley, not being entirely sure what to do with it, how to cook it, if it needed soaking beforehand, and thinking it was more of a 'Waitrose-type' ingredient than something for me. But my mum, who is a Northern-Irish lass, scolded me for my preconceptions, telling me that it was one of the main ingredients in her Irish soup that she would make for herself, her eight brothers and sisters, and her mum and dad. Chastened, I decided to investigate it for myself a few years back, and bought a large bag of it from the supermarket, where it has sat gathering dust on my shelf ever since, until recently, when it has had something of a resurgence in my household.

The chestnuts were a last-minute addition to this – my friend Caroline picked me up some yellow-stickered ones that were a bargainous 20p after Christmas one year – well in date, but being shunted off the supermarket shelves to make way for more seasonal produce – so I put them in here. You can add them if you wish, or leave them out, or swap them for any other kind of nut you fancy or happen to have in.

SERVES 4, GENEROUSLY

1 large onion
1 tbsp cooking oil
6 fat cloves of garlic
200g pearl barley
1 stock cube dissolved in 500ml boiling water or 500ml vegetable stock (see page 218)
salt and pepper
1 tbsp lemon juice or light-coloured vinegar
1 tsp mixed dried herbs
1 x 400g tin of brown lentils
400g mushrooms
180g cooked chestnuts or other nuts (optional)
100g spring greens or other leafy green veg

First peel and finely dice your onion – for ease, you can use frozen onions and put them straight in the pan, making this recipe almost effortless; I interchange between fresh and frozen depending on how I feel on the day, and both are good choices. Add the onion to the pan, and measure in the oil. Peel your garlic cloves and quarter them lengthways, and add to the pot. They will be getting a long, slow cook, and will soften and sweeten along the way, so you can afford to leave them a little on the large side.

Bring to a medium heat on your largest hob ring, and cook for around 5 minutes, stirring intermittently, until they start to soften.

Pour in the pearl barley and stir through, then pour over the stock. In reality, I crumble in the stock cube and pour over the water, and it all turns out fine, but some people like to make the stock in advance and add it. Perhaps it feels a little more like 'proper cooking', but to me it feels like a bit of a faff, so I don't bother.

Bring to the boil, then reduce to a simmer. Add the salt and pepper, lemon juice or vinegar and herbs and stir well, then simmer for 25 minutes, until the water is all absorbed. You will need to stir intermittently to stop the pearl barley from sticking and burning on the bottom of the pan.

Drain and thoroughly rinse your lentils, and add to the pan. Slice your mushrooms finely and add those too.

If you have opted to use chestnuts, crumble some up and leave some whole, and add them here. Fold through, and add another 250ml water. Bring back to the boil, then simmer again for another 15 minutes, until the pearl barley is soft. Finely slice your greens and drop them into the pan a couple of minutes before the end, to soften them but not overcook. If you like your risotto (or barlotto) soupy, you can add a splash more water and stir it in until starchy.

Season with extra black pepper and serve warm.

TO KEEP: Allow to cool completely, then seal in airtight bags, jars or containers. Will keep in the fridge for 3 days or the freezer for 3 months. Heat through completely to serve from frozen, or this can be served chilled from the fridge for a cold lunch or snack.

TIP: *Pearl barley doesn't need soaking, but you can speed up the cooking time by doing so. It absorbs a LOT of water, more so than rice does in a standard risotto, and it takes a little longer to cook. You can enjoy it warm or cold, and it has a sweet, slightly nutty base flavour. It's high in dietary fibre (17g per 100g compared to 0.4g in rice) and protein (12g/100g, whereas rice is 2.7g/100g). It's slightly more expensive than basic rice, but still relatively cheap at 55p for a 500g bag from major supermarkets.*

FROM THE SEA

Fish needn't be expensive when cooking on a budget; tinned sardines are incredibly cheap and extremely nutritious, as well as very versatile. Fish paste and crab paste are staples in my home store cupboard for knocking together a quick pasta sauce or soup, or even folding into instant mash with a little cheese for ultra-budget but very delicious fishcakes. Fish fillets are far cheaper to buy from the freezer department of the supermarket than the fresh counter; simply pop the required number of fillets out of the freezer the night before and put them in a food-safe bag or a bowl in the fridge to defrost, then cook as you would a fresh fillet. There's also a cheeky use for fish fingers in this chapter; because as a parent, and also a longtime fish-finger-sandwich fiend, it's handy to have something to do with something that's incredibly cheap and seemingly always, always in my freezer.

CRAB AND COCONUT BISQUE

I cooked this for lunch for Marina O' Loughlin, the *Sunday Times* restaurant critic, just before the start of the first UK lockdown in 2020. As her identity is kept a closely guarded secret, and is something I have been solemnly sworn not to divulge, cooks and chefs usually have no idea that they're being reviewed until their lunch or dinner appears in the following week's newspaper, ensconced in excoriating wit and enviable quantities of butter. I had no such opportunity for blissful ignorance, and instead spent the night before her arrival sitting bolt upright in bed, rewriting my menu and contemplating doing a runner, or not opening the door, or ordering a KFC bargain bucket with a side of grovelling neurosis. Luckily for me, I pulled myself together, dragged myself into the kitchen, and got so into it I completely ran out of time to do a dessert and ended up thrusting an enormous quantity of M&Ms on the table to round off a five- or six-course lunch. Anyway, Marina liked this dish so much that she asked for the recipe. When the review was published, I ran to my local newsagents and bought a copy of the paper, then read it standing on the pavement outside, totally bowled over by how generous she was with her words and praise. Then I ran back inside and bought a spare copy, in case anything happened to the first. And one for my mum. And one more to pop in a frame. Because I am a ridiculous human being, but also because this was one of the proudest moments of my life. I hope you like it as much as we did.

SERVES 2

1 tbsp light cooking oil

1 large onion

2 celery stalks

1 large carrot

salt and plenty of
   black pepper

1 tbsp garlic (about
   2 cloves)

2 bay leaves (optional)

1 tbsp tomato puree

1 x 75g jar of crab paste

300ml fish or chicken stock

1 x 400ml tin of
   coconut milk

1 tbsp lemon or lime juice

chopped parsley and
   a pinch of chilli, to
   serve (optional)

First heat the oil in a heavy-bottomed saucepan. Peel and dice your onion, slice the celery and dice the carrot, and add to the pan. Season generously. Peel the garlic cloves and halve them lengthways, then add to the pot, along with the bay, if using, and another dash of black pepper.

Cook gently on a medium heat for 10 minutes, stirring intermittently to prevent the veg from sticking and burning.

Add the tomato puree, crab paste and stock, and simmer for 20 minutes, until the veg is very soft.

Transfer everything but the bay leaves to a powerful blender – a small bullet blender is ideal – and add the coconut milk. Blend until smooth, then blend again to catch any tricky bits you might have missed. For extra-silky smoothness, pass it through a fine-mesh sieve, just to be sure.

Add the lemon or lime juice and a grind of pepper, and serve warm, not piping hot. Finish with a smattering of parsley and a pinch of chilli, if you fancy being fancy, but if you don't have either, this soup more than holds its own without any additional fripperies.

TO KEEP: Allow to cool completely, then seal in airtight bags, jars or containers. Will keep in the fridge for 3 days, or the freezer for 3 months.

FISH FINGER KATSU

A deliciously irreverent take on a classic katsu curry, this recipe is an absolute hit with my son and friends, and super simple to make. If you have any pickles kicking about, they make an excellent accompaniment to the sweet and subtly spicy sauce. If you don't, check out page 250 to find out how to rustle some up for next time! Add more or less curry powder depending on the palates of your intended recipients; the coconut milk and sugar temper the heat, but it's easier to add more than it is to try to take it away! I serve this with rice, as possibly the only nod to tradition in the entire recipe, and pop this on to cook at the same time as the sauce goes on the hob.

SERVES 4

1 large onion

2 fat cloves of garlic

a small piece of fresh
     root ginger or 1 tsp
     dried ground ginger

1 tbsp flour

1 chicken or vegetable
     stock cube

2 tsp sugar

1 tsp soy sauce

2 tbsp light cooking oil

400ml full-fat coconut milk

1½ tsp turmeric

1–2 tbsp medium
     curry powder

12 fish fingers

fridge pickles (optional)
     (see page 250 for
     Dustbin Pickles)

First peel and roughly chop your onion, peel your garlic and slice the ginger. Pop these into the large cup of a small bullet blender or a jug blender. Add the flour, stock cube and sugar, then the soy sauce, the oil and finally the coconut milk. Blend everything to a smooth sauce.

Pour the sauce into a saucepan, place on a medium hob ring on a medium heat and add the turmeric and curry powder. Stir in the spices, simmer the sauce for a couple of minutes until it starts to bubble, then transfer it to the smallest hob ring on the lowest heat to continue to thicken and cook.

Meanwhile, as the katsu sauce does its thing, cook your fish fingers according to the packet instructions – usually around 12 minutes. Keep an eye on the sauce and give it a stir every now and then to cook it evenly and prevent it catching on the bottom of the pan.

When the fish fingers are cooked and the sauce is thick and glossy, serve over rice, with pickles if you have them, but don't worry if you don't.

TO KEEP: This doesn't keep well once assembled, but the sauce can be made up to 3 days in advance and stored in a clean jar or food-safe container in the fridge, or up to 6 months in the freezer. Reheat to piping hot to serve.

TIP: I don't put turmeric and curry powder in the blender because they stain the plastic cups of mine, but if you do throw yours into your blender and find it takes on a yellow hue, simply soak the cup in boiling water with a slug of bleach for half an hour until the water cools, and it should be almost as good as new again. Or for a more eco friendly version use a 50/50 vinegar solution (see page 256).

SALT AND VINEGAR SARDINE PASTA

Quick, simple, delicious and a handy standby lunch or dinner for those days when there's just an onion in the fridge and you don't want to have to think too hard about what to do with it.

SERVES 2

1 small onion

160g spaghetti

a few pinches of salt

1 x 120g tin of sardines in oil

black pepper

25ml lemon juice

1 tbsp light-coloured vinegar

a few sprigs of fresh parsley or ½ tsp mixed dried herbs

First peel and finely slice your onion, then set to one side for a moment.

Pop your pasta in a saucepan of generously salted water and bring to the boil. Reduce to a simmer for 8 minutes, or cook according to the packet instructions.

While the pasta is cooking, open your tin of sardines and carefully pour the oil into a non-stick pan. Heat it for a moment, then add the sliced onion and fry for a couple of minutes, then add the sardines. Add a small splash of the salty pasta water – around 2 tablespoons – and plenty of black pepper, then the lemon juice and vinegar. Fry everything together, breaking up the sardines slightly with your wooden spoon or spatula.

While the sardines and onion fry, and the pasta cooks, finely chop your parsley – if using the fresh stuff.

When the pasta is cooked, drain it well and add it to the pan with the sardines and onion. Fry for a further minute all together, then season with plenty more pepper and a pinch of salt. Scatter over the parsley or mixed dried herbs and serve.

TO KEEP: Will keep in the fridge, covered, for 2 days. I stir a tablespoon of mayo through it if there is any left for keeps, to stop the pasta from sticking together and drying out, and also because then it's ideal to enjoy as a cold pasta salad straight from the fridge.

CRAB RAREBIT

A simple lunch that takes just enough effort to feel as though you've done something nice for yourself, but not so much that it's overwhelming. I vary this recipe sometimes and have used anchovies, tuna or tinned mackerel, lightly mashed, in place of the crab paste, and it works a treat however you do it.

SERVES 1–2

2 slices of bread
1 tbsp butter or oil
1 tsp flour
4 tbsp milk
½ tsp mustard – any kind
50g cheese – mild/ mature Cheddar or a nutty red will do
1 small jar of crab or salmon paste
a dash of lemon juice or chilli sauce
black pepper, to taste

Toast the bread lightly, either in a toaster on a low setting or under the grill. Keep the grill on low, if using, otherwise turn the oven on to 160°C/fan 140°C/325°F/gas 3 and ensure there is a shelf in the centre of it.

Melt the butter on a low heat in a small saucepan or heat the oil, and quickly mix in the flour to form a thick paste. Add a tablespoon of milk to loosen it, then a tablespoon more to thin it out. Stir in the mustard and grate in the cheese, and melt it for a minute or two, stirring continuously until it is a thick paste. Add another tablespoon or two of milk as required – it needs to be spreadable but still hold its own.

Spread the crab paste thickly on the bread, then top with the cheese sauce. Add a dash of lemon juice or chilli sauce, whichever you prefer, and season with a little black pepper. Return to the grill or the oven for a couple of minutes, until golden and bubbling. Eat (almost) immediately, allowing a moment for it to cool first!

SARDINESCA

Like a puttanesca sauce but with sardines in place of the anchovies, this simple store-cupboard pasta recipe works well with any strongly flavoured tinned fish. Olives are considerably cheaper if you buy them in jars from the pickles and preserves section of the supermarket than from the fridge aisles – and you get a free jar to boot! (Well, I wouldn't recommend booting it, rather give it a good wash and a dry and use it to store all kinds of useful things.)

SERVES 4

2 x 120g tins of
  sardines in oil
1 x 400g tin of
  chopped tomatoes
200ml vegetable, fish
  or chicken stock
2 tbsp pitted any kind
  olives, finely chopped
1 tbsp lemon juice, or
  any kind of vinegar
salt and black pepper
280g spaghetti or
  other pasta

Tip the sardines into a saucepan, removing any large bones, and mash lightly with a fork. Add the tomatoes, stock and olives, then add the lemon juice or vinegar and plenty of black pepper, and bring to the boil. Turn down the heat and simmer for 30 minutes; you may need to add a splash of water to stop it from drying out.

When the sauce is cooked, remove it from the heat and leave to cool.

Cook the pasta in a pan of plenty of boiling salted water for 8 minutes, or according to the packet instructions. Drain and add to the sauce, and warm through to serve.

TO KEEP: Allow to cool completely, then seal in airtight bags or a lidded container. Will keep in the fridge for 3 days, or freezer for 3 months.

PRAWN COCKTAIL WITH CARAMELIZED GRAPEFRUIT

Frozen prawns are generally the cheapest way to buy them, although I do sometimes find some delightful raw whoppers in the reduced chiller at my local Express store, which makes this much more of a treat! I cannot take credit for the prawns-and-grapefruit combination; I first came across it in a Sophie Grigson recipe some years ago and absolutely adored it, but in order to make this a little more my own, I griddled my grapefruit for a caramel-rich flavour that balances the citrus sharpness beautifully. A great portable picnic piece, starter or light bite that looks and tastes a lot fancier than the sum of its parts.

SERVES 4, GENEROUSLY

200g frozen small prawns

90ml (6 tbsp) seafood sauce

salt and black pepper

1 x 400g tin of grapefruit, about 300g drained weight

½ cucumber

200g cherry tomatoes

130g iceberg lettuce, shredded, or mixed salad leaves

pinch of chilli flakes, some chilli sauce or Tabasco (optional)

Defrost your prawns overnight in the fridge – it's best to do this in the sealed bag they came in to catch the excess liquid that releases as they defrost. If you forget, and we all do, you can leave them in a bowl of cold water, covered, at room temperature, but squeeze one between finger and thumb to make sure it is fully defrosted an hour or so before assembling ready to serve.

Drain your prawns well and gently squeeze out any excess moisture, and transfer to a small bowl. Mix with the seafood sauce and a little salt and pepper, and set to one side. Drain the grapefruit, reserving the juice (see Tip).

Heat a frying pan on a high heat on your largest hob ring – you don't need to add any fat as the grapefruit is super juicy, but if you want to, a splash of oil or a little of any solid fat will do. Carefully place the grapefruit in, spacing it apart so you have room to turn it over, and turn the heat down to medium so it doesn't run riot. Fry the grapefruit segments for 2 minutes on one side, then around a minute and a half on the other, until it starts to char slightly and caramelize. It may take a little longer or be a little quicker depending on your hob and pan – it's almost impossible to be exact about these things as everyone's home kitchens and personal tastes are so variable, so just keep a close eye on it. When done, remove from the heat to cool.

Either finely dice your cucumber or shave it into thin ribbons using a vegetable peeler or julienne peeler. You can also grate it with the large holes on a box grater, if you like, but this tends to produce a 'wetter' end result. If you do it this way, transfer the grated cucumber to a couple of sheets of kitchen roll or a clean flat tea towel and gently squeeze it out to remove any excess liquid.

Quarter your cherry tomatoes, or if you're super fastidious (like me, sometimes) you can cut them into eighths. I quite understand if you don't want to – there's more than enough to be getting on with – but I find it bizarrely meditative.

TIP: *You can use the grapefruit juice from the tin to glaze roasted carrots and parsnips, or as the liquid component in your mincemeat pudding, or add it to festive fizz, if that's your thing, or lemonade if it's not.*

Divide the shredded lettuce between four bowls or glasses. Add the cucumber, then the tomatoes. Dollop in your prawns in seafood sauce, and finish with the cooled griddled grapefruit. Place in the fridge until ready to serve.

If you have some in stock, you may wish to adorn with a little pinch of chilli flakes, some chilli sauce or Tabasco. Lemon isn't needed here, as the grapefruit provides the sharp citrus kick, but a little heat is always a tantalizing finish. If you don't keep these to hand, a little extra pepper will do the same job.

TO KEEP: Can be made in advance and chilled for up to 2 days, or leftovers can be kept for the same amount of time. Not recommended for freezing.

FISH FINGER POCKETS

This recipe has taken many forms over the last year or so; I've made it as crunchy shell tacos, soft little taquitos, in pillowy brioche rolls, but by far the cheapest and most finger-friendly version is these pitta pockets. Pitta breads or flatbreads are remarkably easy to make – see cookingonabootstrap.com for a foolproof if slightly profanely titled recipe – but you can also pick up a packet of half a dozen for around fifty pence at most major supermarkets. (Price correct at the time of writing, those wily corporates are known to change them on a whim, so if it does skyrocket in between me writing this sentence and you seeking some out, I can only apologize for the system of gross capitalism that we all live under and continue to do my best to change it.)

TO SERVE 2 AS A MAIN MEAL OR 4 AS A SNACK

2 wholemeal or white pitta breads

8 small fish fingers

a little lettuce or handful of salad leaves

a handful of grated cheese

1–2 tbsp mayonnaise, to taste

a few sliced pickled radishes or gherkins (optional) (see page 250 for Dustbin Pickles)

For the salsa

1 large tomato, or ½ x 400g tin of chopped tomatoes, well drained

¼ small onion, red or white

a handful of fresh parsley or coriander (optional)

½ tsp mixed dried herbs

a pinch of chilli powder or flakes

1 tsp light-coloured vinegar

1 tsp light cooking oil

salt and pepper

First carefully open your pitta pockets, and halve them across the middle to make four pieces in total. Set these to one side for a moment.

Heat your oven to 220°C/fan 200°C/425°F/gas 7, or turn on your grill to High. If you don't want to put the oven on just for a handful of fish fingers that's entirely understandable – you can fry them over a low heat on the hob for a few minutes each side, but do cut one in half before serving to ensure that it is cooked through! If using the oven, bake in the centre on a baking tray for around 12 minutes or according to the packet instructions.

While the fish fingers are cooking, make your salsa. Either chop your tomato into small dice – around the width of your baby finger – or drain the tinned tomatoes well through a sieve or a colander lined with clean kitchen roll. If using tinned tomatoes, reserve the strained juice in a clean bottle or jar in the fridge and add it to a Bolognese, tomato-based pasta sauce, soup or similar over the next 4 days so as not to waste it.

Finely chop your onion as small as you can get it, and chop your fresh herbs if you're using them. Place the tomato and onion in a small bowl, add the dried herbs, chilli, vinegar, oil, salt and pepper, and stir well to combine. Set this to one side for a moment.

When the fish fingers are cooked, remove them from the oven and insert two into each pocket. Add some salsa, salad and cheese, and a squish of mayo and the pickles if you want them, and, if your oven is on, return them to the oven for a minute or two to melt the cheese and slightly toast the pitta bread.

Serve immediately, and enjoy hot.

FROM THE LAND

Meat products are one of the most expensive parts of a weekly shop, but there are ways to incorporate them without breaking the bank. Chicken wings, thighs and drumsticks all have bags of flavour, with bonus bones for making rich stocks that you don't get from the more expensive skinless, boneless and frankly tasteless chicken breasts. Pork sausages, belly cuts and cooking bacon are usually the cheapest cuts of pig, and you'll find a little black pudding sprinkled throughout this book as well. For beef, tinned stewed steak is surprisingly delicious, and someone else has done the long, slow, tenderizing process for you, meaning it's quick to cook but tastes like it's been stewing for hours. I guess because it has, but just not on your energy bill!

ROAST CHICKEN AND CORONATION SLAW

When I was a child, my mother had a small blackboard in the kitchen with a picture of geese on it that reminded us of the geese my little Greek Aunty Helen had running around her garden in Plymouth. Every weekend, we would sit in the front room and she would assign us all a day of the week on which we could choose what the family had for dinner. As a child, I thought that this was an incredible level of responsibility to have. As an adult who does all of the household shopping and cooking, I sometimes wish I'd had a bigger family so I could do the same!

SERVES 4–6

2 large carrots
½ red cabbage
1 large onion
2 tbsp light-coloured vinegar
a generous pinch of salt and black pepper
oil, for greasing
1 medium chicken (around 1.8kg)
2 tbsp sultanas
a handful of chopped coriander or parsley (optional)

For the dressing
150g mayonnaise
2 tsp curry powder
1 tsp ground turmeric
2 tbsp mango chutney

TIP: *You could use 8 thighs or drumsticks instead of a whole chicken. Reduce the cooking time to 45 minutes, and make sure it is cooked through.*

First make the dressing. Add the mayonnaise, curry powder, turmeric and mango chutney to a bowl. Mix well until evenly combined, then set to one side. The colour will deepen as the turmeric develops.

Grate or julienne your carrots into a large mixing bowl, and finely slice the red cabbage and onion. I use a mandoline to get them super-fine, but you can chop them with a heavy sharp knife and a little patience.

Measure in your vinegar and season generously with salt and pepper. Shake gently to coat the vegetables in the seasoning and vinegar, or rub it in with clean (or gloved) hands to kickstart the macerating process. Stand to one side for 30 minutes so the salt and vinegar start to soften the veg.

While that's happening, lightly oil a roasting tin and pop your chicken into it. Preheat the oven to 190°C/fan 170°C/375°F/gas 5 and ensure there is a shelf at or just below the centre. Season the chicken with salt and pepper to taste, and place the dish in the oven for about 1 hour 10 minutes, or until cooked through according to package instructions. If you're unsure, insert a skewer or small sharp knife into the chubbiest part of the meat and withdraw it slowly; the juices should run clear. If there's any hint of anything pinkish, no matter how faintly, return it to the oven for 10–15 minutes to be on the safe side.

Remove the dressing from the fridge and spoon it over the veg. Mix well to coat the veg. Sprinkle over the sultanas and fold through. Garnish with the coriander or parsley, if using, and extra black pepper. Serve cold, or at room temperature if preferred.

TO KEEP: Will keep in the fridge for up to 3 days in an airtight container. Not recommended for freezing.

FIERY UPSIDE-DOWN
PINEAPPLE CHICKEN

The bromelain in the pineapple, resting on the 'underside' of the upside-down chicken thighs, gently tenderizes the meat as it cooks – giving it a long, slow-cooked feel without much effort. I've also developed a vegan version of this dish using jackfruit and beans. (If you're interested in this, head to my website cookingonabootstrap.com and type 'UPSIDE-DOWN JACKFRUIT' into the search bar to find it!) If you don't have all of the spices to hand, don't buy them in especially, just use what you have and I promise it will still be delicious. I've left out salt from the marinade as soy sauce provides all of the salty lip-smack it needs, but if you want to add some, do feel free.

SERVES 4

1 onion

4 cloves of garlic

a thumb-sized piece of fresh root ginger

1 tsp mixed dried herbs or fresh or dried thyme or rosemary

1 tbsp lemon or lime juice

½ tsp chilli flakes or ¼ tsp hot chilli powder

a few pinches each of ground cinnamon and nutmeg

1 tbsp soy sauce

a good grind of black pepper

a few pinches of white pepper (optional but incredible)

2–4 cloves

2 tbsp light cooking oil

2 tbsp sugar or other sweetener

1 tin of pineapple slices, around 400g

8 skin-on chicken thighs

First peel and dice your onion. Peel and roughly chop the garlic and slice the ginger. Pop it all into the small cup of a bullet blender or food processor, and add the herbs, lemon or lime juice, chilli, cinnamon, nutmeg, soy sauce, black and white pepper (if using), cloves, oil and sugar or other sweetener to taste.

Drain the pineapple over a bowl to collect the juice and transfer the slices to a fridge-safe container, bowl or bag to use in the cooking stage. Add the pineapple juice to the other marinade ingredients and blitz to a smooth paste – you can usually squeeze around 175ml out of a standard-sized tin – how much you need will depend on how large your onion is, so pulse it a few times and have a look at how it's going, then make a judgement for yourself.

When the marinade is made, pop your chicken thighs into a Tupperware with a lid or a sealable freezer bag, and pour it over. Seal tightly and shake generously to coat, then leave to marinate for up to 24 hours – no longer, as the acid in the lemon juice can start to cook the chicken if it hangs around too long! Give it a shake every now and then to re-coat it so all that great flavour gets into every nook and cranny.

When the chicken is marinated, turn your oven on to 190°C/fan 170°C/375°F/gas 5, and transfer the chicken to a tightly fitting roasting dish, skin-side down. The more snug the fit, the more of the marinade is contained around the chicken as it cooks, negating the need to re-baste and keeping your chicken super juicy and full of flavour. Pour all of the marinade evenly over the chicken, and pop a pineapple ring on top of each thigh. Add an extra grind of pepper, then pop the tray in the centre of the oven for 50–60 minutes to cook.

Serve hot, warm or fridge-cold.

TO KEEP: Store in the fridge in a food-safe bag or container for up to 3 days. If freezing, I strongly recommend you strip the chicken from the bones and stir it back into the pineapple and marinade, and store it like that. Defrost thoroughly and heat through to piping hot to serve.

TIP: *If you're minded to make your own stock at some point – for which there is a recipe on page 221 – then pop the bones and any of the less-good bits of chicken into a food-safe bag or container and store them in the freezer until you have accumulated enough to make a stock pot.*

CHEAT 'N' SOUR CHICKEN

My first book, *A Girl Called Jack*, contained a very popular recipe for Diet Coke Chicken, which is still doing the rounds in the wilds of the internet today, much to my delight. Since its publication, several readers got in touch to suggest a riff on sweet and sour chicken using Fanta Orange, and my interest was caught immediately. I scrawled it as a one-line footnote in a recipe notebook and, as so often happens, time ran away with me and the intention to try it remained exactly that. So when I was writing the longlist of recipes for this book, I wrote it down in capital letters, determined to finally give it a go. It took a bit of tweaking to get it right, much to the delight of my son, who absolutely loved it in all its iterations. This, I believe, is the best version of the bunch.

SERVES 4

- 4–6 generous-sized chicken thighs or drumsticks
- 1 very large onion, or 200g frozen onions
- 1 fresh pepper, any colour, or 200g frozen sliced peppers
- 1 small tin of pineapple, chunks or slices, around 200g
- 2 fat cloves of garlic
- a small piece of fresh root ginger
- 1 x 225g tin of water chestnuts, or a handful of thinly sliced broccoli stalk
- 2 tbsp light cooking oil
- a pinch of salt
- plenty of black pepper
- 330ml fizzy orange drink
- 3 tbsp tomato puree or ketchup
- 4 tsp light-coloured vinegar

First, cut the chicken meat from the bones using a small and very sharp knife. Run the blade as close to the bone as possible, almost scraping it along it if you can bear it, to yield the maximum amount of meat for your meal. When done, examine it carefully and feel your way along it with clean hands – you're looking for any gristly, knobbly or rubbery bits – basically, the stuff you don't want to surprise yourself with while tucking into your dinner!

Back to the dinner . . . Peel your onion and dice it nice and chunky, then dice your pepper. Drain the pineapple, reserving the juice to use later, and if you've got rings/slices instead of chunks, chop it up.

Peel and slice your garlic and coarsely grate or finely chop your ginger. Drain the water chestnuts, if using, or finely slice the broccoli stalk if you've opted for that instead.

Heat the oil in a large, non-stick pan. Add the chicken pieces and season with a little salt and pepper, then fry on a high heat for a few minutes, turning occasionally, until the meat is sealed all over.

Add the onion and pepper to the pan, plus the water chestnuts or broccoli stalk, and fry for a further minute. Then add the fizzy orange, pineapple juice, tomato puree or ketchup, and vinegar. Simmer vigorously for around 15 minutes until the sauce reduces and the chicken is cooked through and the veg is tender. Turn the heat down to low for a further 10 minutes until the sauce is thick and glossy, then serve.

TO KEEP: Allow to cool completely then store in the fridge in a food-safe storage bag or container with a lid for up to 3 days. Will keep in the freezer for up to 3 months. Defrost thoroughly, preferably overnight in the fridge, and reheat to piping hot to serve.

CHICKEN IN A CREAMY MUSHROOM SAUCE

Full-fat coconut milk is around half the price of double cream and makes a fine substitute in both sweet and savoury dishes. If you want to reduce the fat content, use reduced-fat coconut milk instead, but you may need to thicken the sauce as it is a great deal runnier than the original. This recipe serves 4, but you can easily change the quantities to feed more or fewer people.

SERVES 4

8 chicken thighs and/ or drumsticks

1 tbsp cooking oil

2 small/medium onions, or 240g frozen onions

400g any kind of mushrooms

400ml full-fat coconut milk

salt and black pepper

200ml chicken stock, allowed to cool

1 tbsp mixed dried herbs

Preheat the oven to 190°C/fan 170°C/375°F/gas 5 and place the chicken in a roasting tin. Cook on the middle shelf for 45 minutes. You don't need to add any oil here, as chicken thighs and drums are quite fatty, so as they warm the fat will seep into the bottom of your roasting dish.

Warm the oil in a large non-stick pan and add the onion and the stalks from the mushrooms, reserving the caps. Cook on medium heat for 5 minutes to soften, then transfer to a blender with the coconut milk and stock and blend until smooth. Pour the liquid back into your pan and add the mushroom caps. Cook on low heat on a medium hob ring while the chicken is roasting. Season to taste, then stir through the mixed dried herbs.

When the chicken is cooked, add it to the sauce and mushrooms. Season generously with black pepper and serve.

TO KEEP: To store, strip the chicken from the bones and discard the bones (see tip about saving to make stock on page 161). Fold the chicken back through the mushrooms and sauce, and store in the fridge in an airtight container for 2 days or freeze for 3 months. Defrost thoroughly overnight in the fridge, and reheat until piping hot throughout to serve.

PORK, HERB AND WHITE BEAN MEATBALLS

Using white beans to pad out mince is a trick I have been doing for years, learned in poverty and continued as a frugality that became second nature in the kitchen. It is an economical way to make a small amount of minced meat go further; and it makes for juicy, soft, tender meatballs that still pack a protein punch. I find the beans somewhat temper the flavour, so you can add a pinch of gravy granules to beef it back up again or, as I have done here, add herbs and spices to bolster it. These are great served in a tomato sauce with pasta or served with rice and greens.

MAKES 36 GENEROUS-SIZED MEATBALLS TO SERVE 6

2 x 400g tins of cannellini beans

500g pork mince or sausages, squeezed from their skins

1 large onion, roughly chopped

1 tbsp mixed dried herbs

salt and pepper, to taste

oil, for frying

Drain the beans and blitz together with all the other ingredients (except the oil) in a food processor until combined but still chunky. Shape into meatballs approx. 30g each. I weigh the first few to get an idea of size, then do it from sight – you can guess straight off, but you may not get the full 36 if you do!

Preheat the oven to 180°C/fan 160°C/350°F/gas 4 and place a large roasting tin nearby.

Heat a splash of oil in a large, wide, non-stick pan and place the meatballs in – you may need to cook them in batches. Cook for 3 minutes then turn them over gently. Cook for 2 minutes more, then transfer to the roasting tin. Repeat until all the meatballs are in the tin.

Bake the meatballs in the centre of the oven for 18 minutes until browned and cooked through, shaking the tin gently halfway through to stop them from sticking and burning.

TO KEEP: Will keep in the fridge for 3 days or the freezer for 3 months. You can freeze the mixture, either as a lump or in balls, and defrost completely before making and cooking the meatballs.

QUICK SAUSAGE AND STUFFING BOLOGNESE

I mince my mushrooms and carrots for this recipe to make them less detectable for fussy palates, and to make the sausagemeat go further. This recipe, if divided by four, provides three and a half of your five a day. The stuffing may seem a bizarre addition, but it imparts a herby flavour and imitates the texture of mince, making a little of the most expensive ingredient go much, much further.

SERVES 4, GENEROUSLY

6 sausages

1 medium onion or 160g onion – frozen is fine

1 tbsp cooking oil

320g mixed mushrooms

320g carrots (optional)

1 tbsp garlic paste or chopped fresh garlic

1 x 400g tin of chopped tomatoes

120ml black tea, red wine or 1 red wine stock cube and 120ml water

1 tbsp mixed dried herbs

2 tbsp sage and onion stuffing

salt and pepper, to taste

First, squeeze the sausagemeat from the skins – you can either do it by squeezing them in the middle and pushing it out, or by cutting the sausage from top to bottom on one side with kitchen scissors and peeling the skin away – both methods are fairly quick and simple. Peel and dice your onion. Add the meat to a large non-stick pan, with the onion and a splash of oil. Bring to a low heat on a medium hob ring.

Roughly chop your mushrooms and carrots (if using) and mince them in a small bullet blender or food processor. If you don't have either, you can grate your carrots and chop your mushrooms by hand. Transfer the veg to the pan and stir in the garlic or garlic paste. Turn the heat up to high for 2 minutes, stirring to disturb and combine the ingredients.

Pour over the chopped tomatoes and the black tea, red wine or stock, then add the herbs and stuffing. Stir well, cover the pan with a lid, and reduce the heat to a simmer. Simmer for 20 minutes, until the sausagemeat is cooked and the veg is soft.

TO KEEP: Will keep for 3 days in the fridge, cooled and stored in an airtight container, or 3 months in the freezer. Defrost completely before reheating to piping hot throughout to serve. Once defrosted, do not refreeze.

TOAD AND FRIENDS

A comforting classic that can be made easily with vegetarian sausages, if you like. My Small Boy loves this for his dinner, and so did I when I was his age! And now, with a little supervision and encouragement, he delights in making this himself sometimes, sitting in front of the oven door watching the batter rise and exclaiming delightedly to himself about it every time. I hope he is always so filled with such simple joy, but for now, I treasure these moments and the soft sticky wonderment of his youth.

SERVES 4–6, GENEROUSLY

2 large carrots
2 large parsnips
1 large onion or 2 tiddlers
a handful of Brussels
    sprouts
2 tbsp cooking oil
6 sausages
100g plain flour
a pinch of salt
1 egg
300ml milk

First bring a generously salted pan of water to the boil. Quarter your carrots lengthways, and your parsnips, and peel and cut your onion into wedges. Carefully drop them into the boiling water and cook for around 8 minutes, just long enough to start to soften but retain a little bite, as they will continue to cook in the oven. Add the sprouts halfway through, so they cook for around 4 minutes.

While your veg softens, preheat the oven to 200°C/fan 180°C/400°F/gas 6 and grab a roasting dish around 25 x 30cm, or a deep round cake tin will do the same job. Pop the oil and sausages into the tin and cook for around 10 minutes, giving it a jostle halfway through to make sure they cook evenly.

While all that is going on, get a mixing bowl. Add the flour, salt, egg and half the milk. Beat them together to form a smooth batter. Pour in the rest of the milk and continue to beat until very smooth.

Remove the roasting tin from the oven and add your veg. Pour in the batter carefully. Move the sausages and veg with a fork or clean finger so they are roughly evenly distributed. Bake for 40 minutes until the batter is risen and golden. DO NOT OPEN THE OVEN DOOR until the 40 minutes are over, else your batter will deflate!

Serve with gravy, immediately. You may up the veg count for this to make it an all-in-one meal, if you like.

TO KEEP: Will keep in the fridge for 2 days, or the freezer for 3 months. Defrost completely and warm through in a low oven to serve.

CANNELLINI, LEEK AND SAUSAGE PASTA

This one came about when my friends John and Caroline were at my house, helping put up some shelves and provide moral support while I sorted out my endless paperwork, and they both needed to be fed. I have a running list on the front of the fridge sometimes that has the dates of the week on it, and by each is written anything that needs using up imminently. It helps me keep track of use-by dates in the fridge without endlessly rummaging, and it also takes some of the pressure of meal-planning off, as half the decisions are already made for me! The little nudging note said 'cabbage and leeks' on this day, but John is a robust and lively fellow who cannot live on greenery alone, and there was half a packet of sausages that needed to be used too, so this was born. And according to my two testers, it was absolutely delicious. 'You should put that in a book,' said John. And he's usually right about these things, so I did.

SERVES 4

1 medium onion, or 160g frozen onions

4 fat cloves of garlic

2 tbsp cooking oil

500ml chicken or vegetable stock (see page 218 for homemade)

a pinch of salt

1 x 400g tin of cannellini beans

½ tsp mustard (any kind)

1 tsp mixed dried herbs

6 sausages

300g pasta

160g leeks

160g green cabbage or spring greens

black pepper

TIP: Kitchen scissors make it an absolute breeze to finely slice the sausages.

First peel and dice your onion, if using a fresh one, and toss into a large non-stick pan. Peel and finely chop the garlic and add that too. Measure in 1 tablespoon of the oil and cook on a low heat for a couple of minutes to start to soften the onion and garlic. Pour over the stock and add a scant pinch of salt, then bring to the boil.

Drain and thoroughly rinse your cannellini beans and add to the pan, along with the mustard and herbs. Reduce to a simmer and cook for around 30 minutes, until the beans are soft and creamy.

Meanwhile, in a separate pan, heat the other tablespoon of oil and fry the sausages for 10 minutes, turning a couple of times to evenly brown all the way around. Remove from the heat and slice thinly, around half a centimetre if you can manage it (see Tip), then add to the pan of beans for the remainder of the cooking time.

After 30 minutes have passed, measure the pasta into the pan and add 300ml water. Stir well and bring to the boil, then reduce to a simmer and cook for 10 minutes more.

Finely slice the leeks and cabbage and throw them into the pot for a few minutes to soften, then serve with plenty of black pepper to finish.

TO KEEP: This will keep in the fridge for up to 3 days, and is delicious fridge-cold, lukewarm or piping hot, but I wouldn't recommend for freezing unless you stir through a loose cheesy sauce (see page 247). It will freeze for 3 months.

SAUSAGE AND CHICKPEA CURRY

An alternative use for sausages and chickpeas that is a hit with adults and children alike.
The spice level here is fairly mild, so feel free to ramp it up a little if you like it a little wilder.

SERVES 4

1 large onion

4 fat cloves of garlic
or 6 dinky ones

2 tbsp cooking oil

6 sausages

a thumb-sized piece
of root ginger

1 tbsp ground cumin

1 tsp ground turmeric

1 tbsp garam masala

a pinch of chilli flakes

1 x 400g tin of chickpeas

1 x 400g tin of tomatoes

1 x 400g tin of full-
fat coconut milk

scant ½ tsp English mustard

salt and black
pepper, to taste

a handful of spinach,
kale or spring greens

Peel your onion and quarter it, then cut each quarter segment in half. If you have onion-averse household members, feel free to chop it much smaller to sneak past them, but I like it nice and chunky to complement the pieces of sausage in the dish. Peel the garlic cloves and quarter them lengthways.

Heat the oil in a large non-stick pan, add the onions and garlic and then the sausages. Grate in the ginger and turn the heat down to medium–low. Add the spices – the cumin, turmeric, garam masala and chilli flakes – and stir in to coat the onions evenly. Cook on a low–medium heat for around 10 minutes, stirring intermittently to keep it all moving so it doesn't stick and burn.

Drain and thoroughly rinse your chickpeas and add to the pan. Pour over the tomatoes and coconut milk, add your mustard and stir well. Bring to the boil, then reduce to a simmer and cook, uncovered, for 25 minutes.

Season to taste with a little salt and pepper, and fold the spinach through to wilt before serving.

TO KEEP: Will keep in the fridge for 3 days, or the freezer for 3 months. Defrost completely and reheat piping hot to serve.

SPICY PORK BELLY WITH PRUNE CHUTNEY

This recipe is a bit of a showstopper favourite of mine; the spicy flavours of the pork and the sweet, sticky chutney combine to make a truly memorable, special-occasion meal, without having to raid the piggy bank.

SERVES 4–6

1 x 425g tin of
    prunes in juice
2 fat cloves of garlic
1 tbsp light-coloured
    vinegar – cider, red,
    white or rice are
    all fine, plus 1 tbsp
    for the chutney
1 tbsp light cooking oil
½ tsp ground cinnamon
1 tsp fennel seeds
1 tsp mixed dried herbs
a pinch of chilli flakes
½ tsp coarse salt or
    ¼ tsp table salt
plenty of black pepper
800g pork belly, sliced
1 large onion
2 large celery stalks

First strain your prunes, separating the juice into a large jar with a lid. Set the prunes to one side while you make the marinade for the pork.

Peel and crush or mince your garlic and add to the juice, along with the vinegar and the oil. Mix together the cinnamon, fennel, herbs, chilli and salt and pepper – you can chop the fennel seeds with a large heavy knife or crush them in a pestle and mortar if you like, but leaving them whole works fine, too. Add most of this seasoning to the marinade jar, keeping a little to one side. Tightly screw the lid onto the jar and shake well to mix and emulsify the marinade. Pop the pork into the smallest food-safe sealable bag or container that will hold it, and pour three-quarters of the marinade carefully all over. Refrigerate for 6–24 hours, but no longer.

While the pork is marinating, it's time to make the accompanying chutney. De-stone the prunes by gently squeezing them – the stones should pop right out. Discard the stones and pop the prunes into a medium saucepan. Peel and halve, then very finely slice your onion and celery. Add to the pan along with the remaining marinade and an extra tablespoon of vinegar.

Bring to the boil, then reduce to a simmer and cook until the veg is very soft. You may need to add a splash of water here and there, so keep an eye on it and make sure it doesn't dry out, but it should take around 25 minutes depending on the size of your pan, whether it has a lid on and how finely your veg was chopped. Remove from the heat and transfer to a very clean jar. If you're planning on keeping it for longer than a fortnight, you should use a sterilized jar (see page 90) – but any less than that a very clean one should be fine. Screw the lid on while it's hot, and leave to cool completely before labelling and popping in the fridge.

When it's time to cook the pork, remove it from the fridge for 20 minutes to come to room temperature, and preheat your oven to 210°C/fan 190°C/410°F/gas 6, ensuring there is a shelf in the centre of it or just below.

Transfer the pork to the smallest roasting dish or tin that will hold it – this packs the marinade in tightly around it, meaning the flavours can permeate throughout the cooking process, and it keeps the meat tender and juicy. Pour the marinade in to just below where the top fat layer starts – you want to keep this exposed to the hot air in the oven so it crisps up. Rub the remaining salt-and-spice seasoning onto the exposed fat, working it in with your fingers or a pastry brush.

Pop your pork belly in for 10–12 minutes to crisp the fat to crackling. Turn the heat down to 140°C/fan 120°C/275°F/gas 1 and cook for a further 90 minutes.

Place a wire cooling rack on top of a roasting tray or baking tray with sides for when the pork is ready. Remove from the oven and place each piece on the wire rack to rest for 10 minutes before serving.

You can make the leftover juices into a gravy by quickly combining 1 tablespoon each of oil or butter and flour in a small saucepan over a low heat. Gradually add the juices, stirring the whole time, and thin with a little stock or water as desired. Taste and season, then serve hot – it will thicken as it cools. Alternatively, you can use them as the base for a casserole or stew with any leftover pork, beans and root vegetables – it's far too good to waste!

TO KEEP: Leftovers will keep in the fridge, well covered, for up to 3 days. You can freeze the pork belly for up to 3 months; defrost thoroughly and reheat to piping hot to serve. The chutney will keep for 4–6 weeks in the fridge.

CORNED BEEF CHILLI

This is a meal that my family regularly enjoys, and the recipe can be adapted easily to suit a range of preferences – for example, I sometimes swap the corned beef for stewed steak for a dish that tastes properly luxurious with even less effort. If you decide to take this route, do add the gravy from the stewed steak tin as well, as it disappears into the base of the chilli and adds a real extra layer of deliciousness. This might seem surprising, considering it doesn't generally look that appealing in its tinned state, but with a little help from some spices and store-cupboard basics, it's a real treat.

SERVES 6

1 small onion

6 large cloves of garlic

2 tbsp vegetable or olive oil

salt and black pepper

2 tbsp paprika, sweet or smoked

2 tbsp ground cumin

1 x 400g tin of kidney beans

1 x 400g tin of cannellini beans

2 x 400g tins of chopped tomatoes

200ml strong black tea, or red wine

1 tbsp tomato puree or ketchup

20g dark chocolate

1 x 350g tin of corned beef

grated cheese, mash or cooked rice, to serve

First peel and finely slice your onion, then peel and chop the garlic.

Heat the oil in a large saucepan over a medium heat and add the onion and garlic. Season with a little salt and plenty of pepper. Cook for a few minutes until slightly softened, then add the paprika and cumin and stir in to coat the veg.

Drain and rinse both tins of beans and add to the pan, along with the tomatoes, tea or wine, tomato puree or ketchup and the dark chocolate, broken into chunks. Cook, stirring gently, for 5–6 minutes.

Dice your corned beef and add to the pan, stirring it in. Cook for a further 20 minutes until the beef has basically melted into the sauce and the chilli is thick and a rich red-brown colour. Serve with a pile of grated cheese, and mash or rice.

TO KEEP: This will keep in the fridge for 3 days or in the freezer for up to 3 months. Defrost thoroughly before reheating to piping hot to serve.

HUMBLE SAUSAGE PIE

This is a very simple recipe for days when you really need some kind of warm comfort but you're absolutely spent. It can be customized to use whatever you have in the cupboard; I've made it over the years with sausages, bacon, chicken, mushrooms, tofu, hot dog sausages, diced Spam and corned beef – all separately, and all good in their own way. It's extremely versatile in its simplicity, so use what you have or what you fancy – hopefully they're the same thing! I am rather fastidious about the use of the term 'pie'; it needs to have walls, a base and a lid in order to qualify, but if you are in a hurry, or less pernickety, a casserole-with-a-hat will just about pass muster.

SERVES 6

300g sausages
cooking oil, for frying
1 small onion (around 100g chopped weight)
300g mixed frozen vegetables
1 x 400g tin of white beans
4 tbsp gravy granules
flour, for dusting
400g shortcrust pastry, from a packet or homemade
1 egg, to glaze (optional) or use milk, oil and soy sauce

First, finely slice your sausages. Heat a little oil in a frying pan and add the sausage 'coins'. Fry for around 6 minutes to seal, jostling and turning them over so they brown lightly on both sides.

Peel and finely slice or dice your onion and add to the pan, along with the veg. Drain and thoroughly rinse the beans, then add those too. Stir in the gravy granules and pour over around 350ml water, then gently warm on a medium heat for around 5 minutes, stirring, until the veg starts to defrost and the gravy thickens. Take off the heat and set to one side for a moment.

Lightly grease a 25cm pie dish or other suitable implement, and lightly dust your worktop with flour. Roll out the pastry until it is a few millimetres thick, and then, in one swift but supportive movement, pick it up and transfer it to the pie tin, making sure it generously overlaps the edges. Gently press it into the seams and corners, if there are any, taking care not to tear it. This can be awkward, so if you aren't particularly confident about it, use the ready-rolled stuff instead, which holds its own marvellously for the novice cook.

When the dish is lined, carefully cut away the excess pastry from the edges and press into a ball. You will use this to make the lid in a moment.

Gently add the filling to the pie, one spoon at a time. It is tempting to simply dump the lot into the pan, but the sheer force of almost a kilo of veg and beans and gravy may rip your pastry to shreds, so take your time with it, easing it in, until the pie is filled to the very top.

Roll out the remaining pastry to a piece large enough to cover the pie, then place it carefully on top. Trim away the edges (you can make these into miniature pies in a muffin tin, or little tartlets with a dollop of jam), then seal the edges by gently pressing them together with the tines of a fork.

If you are using an egg, beat it and brush it over the top. If you don't have one, a little milk (ordinary or plant-based) shaken with a little oil and a drop of soy sauce will give the same glazed effect.

Pop it in the oven at 180°C/fan 160°C/350°F/gas 4 for 45 minutes, or until golden. It's pretty simple, but it's unmistakably a pie.

TO KEEP: Will keep in the fridge for 3 days, or the freezer for 3 months. Defrost completely and warm through in a low oven to serve.

A GIRL CALLED JACK
JACK MONROE

A YEAR IN 120 RECIPES

The Royal Marsden CANCER COOKBOOK

JACK MONROE

CUCINARE CON 2 €URO AL GIORNO

#CookForSYRIA
RECIPE BOOK

COOKING ON A BOOTSTRAP JACK MONROE

JACK MONROE TIN CAN COOK C

JACK MONROE Vegan (ish)

JACK MONROE GOOD FOOD for BAD DAYS

GOOD SWEETS

COLD MEAT

The Art of Home Cookery
AMBROSE HEATH FABER

OPEN SESAME

SAUSAGE, BACON AND MANY-VEG CASSEROLE

This recipe was originally designed to fulfil five out of five of our five a day, making three portions, but it made such a large pan that I easily got four portions out of it, one each for tonight and one each for the freezer for another day, which means each of the veg portions is now slightly shy of the recommended 70g per person, but it's still a hearty dose of a mixture of vitamins and minerals in one simple pan.

My Small Boy, who at 12 years old with dinner plates the same size as my own these days cannot be described as 'Small' for much longer, declared this one of his favourite dinners and offered to help me make it next time. Possibly only because I batted him out of the kitchen for trying to pilfer a sausage, but perhaps because he's developing an enthusiasm for cookery as well.

SERVES 4

210g onion
210g carrot
200g mushrooms
2 fat cloves of garlic
1 tbsp lard or cooking oil
6–8 sausages
500ml boiling water
2 tsp gravy granules
20g tomato puree
1 chicken stock cube
2 tbsp mixed dried herbs
100g bacon
400g baked beans, including sauce
2 tbsp dried stuffing crumbs
a splash of vinegar
plenty of black pepper

First peel and dice your onion, then dice your carrots – don't worry about peeling those, the skin is full of fibre and goodness, but if they're a bit grubby give them a good gentle scrub to dislodge any stubborn earth. Dice your mushrooms. Set all the veg aside for a moment.

Peel and finely slice your garlic and set to one side.

Heat the lard or cooking oil in a very large non-stick pan and add the sausages. Cook for 5–6 minutes on a medium–high heat to seal them, and also to release some extra fat into the pan.

When the sausages are sealed, add your veg. Reduce the heat to medium and cook for 4–5 minutes, nudging it all around with a spatula or wooden spoon to prevent it from sticking and burning. Don't add the garlic just yet as it may burn.

Boil the kettle, and measure your gravy granules and tomato puree into a heatproof jug. If you don't have one, a large mug will do, but you will need to add another mug of water to the pan later on. Crumble in the stock cube and add the herbs. Pour over the boiling water and stir well to make a rich and delicious sauce for your base. The gravy granules thicken it and add a depth of flavour, and the tomato puree is for colour and a slight sweetness. You don't need to add any extra salt to this dish, due to the salt in the stock cube and the gravy, which is why I didn't season the veg above. I am painfully aware my palate for salinity is quite a greedy one, but I managed to resist here!

Chop the bacon and add to the veg pan, stirring intermittently for a minute, then add the garlic and stir briefly for a minute to knock the acerbic edge off it, then pour over the jug of sauce. Stir in the baked beans, including the sticky orange sauce – the sweetness of it disappears into this dish and balances it out beautifully, so if you are using beans without sauce in, add a pinch of sugar and a little extra tomato puree to counter its omission.

Bring the pan to the boil, then reduce to a simmer. Place a lid on if you have one and simmer for 30–40 minutes, adding a splash more water if necessary, and stirring every now and again. Around 10 minutes before serving, add the stuffing crumbs, a splash of vinegar and a generous amount of black pepper.

TO KEEP: Will keep in the fridge for 2 days, or the freezer for 3 months. Defrost completely and warm through in the microwave or a pan on the hob until piping hot to serve.

TIP: *I like to add in a few large rainbow chard leaves. You can also use spinach, kale, spring greens or dark green cabbage if you wish, fresh or frozen, or leave it out. (Ha! 'Leaf' it out.)*

SWEET TREATS

Being on a tight food budget or being frugal with your food and shopping, whether by choice or not, doesn't have to mean a life of penury and misery. The puddings chapters in my cookbooks are always by far the largest, because I believe that life is to be enjoyed and self-care is paramount; and one of the ways I show love is through baking. Even — or perhaps most importantly — if it's just for me.

TINNED PEACH DRIZZLE CAKE

This recipe can be made with any tinned fruit; pears also work particularly well, but I do love the tropical decadent sweetness of peaches and their incredible colour.

SERVES 8

250g butter or baking spread, plus extra for greasing

1 x 425g tin of peach slices

200g finely ground white sugar

3 medium eggs

250g self-raising flour, or 250g plain flour plus 1 tbsp baking powder

a pinch of salt

100g icing sugar

Preheat the oven to 180°C/fan 160°C/350°F/gas 4, and lightly grease a 900g loaf tin.

Strain the peaches through a colander or sieve set over a bowl or jug to catch the juices, pressing the slices lightly against the sieve to extract as much of the juice as possible. Set the juice to one side – you'll be using it for the icing later!

If using butter, dice it into 1cm cubes and leave them in a bowl at room temperature for 20–30 minutes to soften, or use the large holes of a grater to grate it cold from the fridge. If using a spread, it should mix together easily. In a large mixing bowl, cream together your butter or baking spread with the sugar. Mix well with a wooden spoon or sturdy silicone spatula until well combined, to form an even buttercream.

Break in one egg and mix well, using a fork to combine it with the buttercream mixture, then repeat the same process with the other two eggs.

Add the baking powder (if using plain flour) and a pinch of salt, then add the flour a quarter at a time, mixing well to combine evenly each time before adding the next lot.

Finally, tip in the drained peaches and stir in – they will carry some residual juice that will pool at the edges of your batter, so mix this in well, but try not to break up the soft peach slices too much in the process.

When the batter is even and smooth, pour it into your prepared tin, jostling the peach slices so that they are evenly distributed throughout. Bake in the centre of the oven for 50–60 minutes, until risen and golden and a small sharp knife inserted into the middle comes out clean. If it comes out with some batter attached, turn the oven down to 140°C/fan 120°C/275°F/gas 1 and check every 10 minutes until done.

Remove the tin carefully from the oven and stand it on a wire cooling rack. Loosen the edges with a sharp knife or palette knife, and leave the cake in the tin for 30 minutes to firm and cool. Turn out onto the rack for a further hour to cool enough to ice it – it may take longer depending on the temperature of your kitchen. (You want to be able to touch it with your fingertips for a few

seconds and not register that it's warm, otherwise the icing will slither down the sides and you end up with more of a glaze. Still delicious, but not what we're going for.)

When the cake is cool, sift the icing sugar into a large mixing bowl and add 1 tablespoon of the reserved peach juice. Mix well to make a smooth, thick icing. Pop the cake and wire rack on top of a clean baking tray with sides, or a roasting tin, and drizzle the icing over the top. Leave it to set for a few minutes, then scrape up the icing that has fallen through the wire rack back into the bowl and repeat the process. Leave to set for 30 minutes, then enjoy.

TO KEEP: Leftovers will keep for up to 4 days in an airtight container in a cool dark place, or 4 months in the freezer. If you are freezing it, it is best frozen in slices so they can be easily defrosted whenever you fancy a quick treat!

CHOCOLATE PRUNE PUDDING

Chocolate and prunes are a delicious combination, but for those of you who aren't keen on the little purple juicy fruits, you can use tinned mandarins or pears in this instead.

SERVES 6

1 x 400g tin of prunes

75g applesauce from a jar

75g sugar

150g dark chocolate, broken into chunks

75ml oil, plus extra for greasing

200ml full-fat coconut milk

175g self-raising flour

1 tsp (4g) bicarbonate of soda

1 tbsp (8g) ground dried orange peel

First, drain the prunes and reserve the juice – you'll be using that for the chocolate sauce in a bit. Remove the stones from the prunes by giving them a gentle squeeze between finger and thumb – they should just pop right out. Discard the stones – I am yet to find a use for them, so if you know of one, do get in touch and tell me!

Pop the prunes into a saucepan with a splash of the reserved juice, the applesauce and all of the sugar, and cook on a low heat for 15 minutes, stirring vigorously every now and then to break them down and make a chunky, glossy, not-quite jam.

Remove from the heat and stir in 110g chocolate to melt it, then add the oil and the coconut milk. It doesn't look too brilliant at this stage, but it gets better, I promise! Measure in the flour, bicarb and orange peel, and stir well to form a smooth, glossy cake batter.

Preheat the oven to 180°C/fan 160°C/350°F/gas 4 and lightly grease a 450g loaf tin. Pour in the mixture and bake in the centre of the oven for 45 minutes, until risen and a small sharp knife inserted into the centre comes out clean. Remove from the oven but leave in the tin for 20 minutes to cool and firm up.

While the cake is cooling, bring a small pan of water to the boil, with a heatproof bowl balanced on top. Make sure the bottom of the bowl isn't touching the water.

Break up the remaining 40g chocolate and add to the bowl to melt it slowly, stirring it to speed up the process. Gradually add the remaining reserved prune juice, stirring it in, to make a sauce.

Pierce the cake all over with a cocktail stick, skewer or small sharp knife while still in the tin, and pour the sauce over. Let it sink into the cake and serve warm.

STICKY LEMON PUDDING

This recipe came about one afternoon when I couldn't decide between making myself a sticky toffee pudding – classic in its stodgy, saccharine comfort blanket – or a lemon drizzle – zesty and bright with its promise of sunny afternoons. So I took to the trusty barometer of reason, Twitter, to ask for help. The poll came back as a 52/48 split, and we all know how contentious those are, so in order to try to satisfy both sides of the pudding referendum, I mashed the two options together. The sticky warm component structure of toffee pudding with the flavour profile of a rich lemon drizzle cake. I wasn't sure it would work (but I was willing to give it as many goes as was necessary for the name of, uh, research), but to my delight, it came out perfectly first time.

SERVES 6, GENEROUSLY

For the pudding

70g baking spread, plus extra for greasing

100g sugar

100ml milk

2 medium eggs

¾ tsp bicarbonate of soda

130g self-raising flour

1 tbsp lemon juice

160g mixed citrus peel or mixed dried fruits

For the topping

100g lemon curd

2 tbsp (28g) baking spread or butter

splash of cream (optional)

40g mixed citrus peel or mixed dried fruits

Preheat the oven to 180°C/fan 160°C/350°F/gas 4 and lightly grease your tin (roughly 18cm – either a round cake tin or a brownie tin will work).

Weigh the baking spread into a large mixing bowl and add the sugar. Beat together until well combined – use a masher or a fork to get the spread started if it's come straight from the fridge; this is where a cheap baking block comes into its own as it never quite solidifies in the way that good-quality butter does, making it perfect for the impatient baker. Add the milk a little at a time, mixing in well to form a smooth creamy paste. Crack in the eggs one at a time and beat well to combine. It may look a little split or sloppy here, don't worry about that, the flour will pull it back together in a moment.

Add the bicarb and mix in well to evenly distribute, then add the flour. When it forms a smooth and even batter, add the lemon juice a little at a time, then fold in the mixed peel. Pour into your greased tin and place in the centre of the oven. Bake for 30 minutes or until risen and lightly golden.

While the pudding is cooking, make the topping. Spoon the lemon curd and baking spread or butter into a small heavy-bottomed saucepan and place on a low heat on the smallest hob ring. Stir as the curd starts to bubble and the butter melts, then remove from the heat. If you are feeling extra indulgent, and you happen to have some kicking around, add a splash of cream as it comes off the heat as a nod to the original sticky toffee pudding. This is by no means essential – the whole thing is rich enough without it. Set the sauce to one side to cool.

When the pudding is risen and golden, remove carefully from the oven. Poke around twelve holes into it with a small sharp knife, skewer or cocktail stick, and pour the sauce on top. Sprinkle the 40g peel over, and carefully tilt the tin from side to side so the sauce coats the whole top and starts to sink into the holes.

Allow to cool and soak for an agonizing 15–20 minutes, enjoying the heady citrus aroma that will permeate your home in the meantime, then dig right in.

TO KEEP: Keeps in an airtight container or food-safe bag in a cool, dry place for up to 3 days.

BREAD AND JAM ICE CREAM

In the name of thorough research, I tested and tasted this recipe many, many times. My relationship with bread and jam is one that is fraught with strange feelings (see over the page for more on this), but I promise you don't need to have your own traumatic association to justify making this; it stands alone as an excellent treat for all occasions and none.

SERVES AROUND 8–10

100g white bread (stale or fresh)

200ml whole milk

3 egg yolks

100g finely ground sugar

300ml double cream

8 tbsp red jam

2 tsp breadcrumbs (stale or fresh)

1 tsp sugar

a few pinches of vanilla (optional)

TIP: *You could pop the leftover drained milk in a jar in the fridge and use it within a day or so to make a cheese sauce recipe (see page 247).*

First tear your bread into pieces, and place them in a bowl. Pour over the milk and stand it to one side for an hour or so to soak.

Beat the egg yolks in a large mixing bowl until pale and fluffy. Add the sugar slowly, continuing to beat it well.

Pour in the cream slowly and whisk firmly and steadily until the mixture has almost doubled in size. Run a clean finger through: it should feel airy, light and fluffy, and not fall off your finger. A common mistake is to beat too hard, knocking the air out of it as quickly as you beat it in – you want a firm and rhythmic hand, but not too much vigour. It should stand in soft peaks when you lift your whisk out. If you scrimp on this step, your ice cream will set rock hard, and while it won't be entirely unpleasant, it will be a bit more difficult to eat.

Drain the milk from the bread, give the pieces a gentle squeeze and tear them into smaller pieces. Fold these through the whipped-cream mixture, then dollop in the jam a tablespoon at a time, being careful not to break it up too much.

Pour it into a 900ml loaf tin or plastic container. Mix together the breadcrumbs, sugar and vanilla, if using, and scatter over the top. Cover the container with a lid or cling film to seal, then freeze for at least 4 hours.

Remove from the freezer 5 minutes before serving, to allow it to soften a little, and return it to the freezer once served to reset.

TO KEEP: It will keep in the freezer for up to 4 months.

AN EXTRA HELPING

As a single mother on the dole some years ago now, I wrote a blog post called 'Hunger Hurts' that accidentally went viral, which was about the day-to-day realities of scraping by with handfuls of thin air and nothing.

While the glossy media-endorsed version of my life is one of plucky adversity and magic meals for pennies, in reality for many more days than I've been able to admit until I've been far enough away from it to look back properly, I would eat cheap white bread from the bag, eyeballing my infant son's dinner plate, hoping he would leave something for me to swish my piece of bread around in and flavour it with.

I ate a lot of bread and jam in those days, because it was cheap and easy, and required no mental or emotional labour nor fuel to prepare. I could store it without the unplugged fridge, and it swiftly yet temporarily silenced a hunger pang with stodge and sweetness.

After my first book came out, and for a long time after that, I couldn't face even the thought of bread and jam. What had once been a joyous childhood staple now triggered a shudder of feelings I wasn't ready to examine. It's taken almost a decade to start to unpack that box, and as part of my healing process, one therapist suggested to me that I work 'bread and jam' into something positive, to reframe how I thought and felt about it. I laughed, but he was onto something. And so Bread and Jam Ice Cream was born. And I have nothing but overwhelmingly positive feelings about it. It hasn't vanquished all of my mental demons from that era, but it feels like a pretty good place to start.

CORNFLAKE ICE CREAM

Making ice cream needn't be a chore – this family favourite is just three ingredients and the work of a moment, with no specialist equipment needed. It also works with other cereals, including Coco Pops, cornflakes and Cinnamon Grahams. Feel free to experiment with your favourite cereals!

SERVES 4

120g Crunchy Nut cornflakes or standard plain variety

100g full-fat coconut milk

1 x 397g tin of condensed milk

First tip the cornflakes into the blender, along with the coconut milk and condensed milk. Make sure you scrape out the condensed milk tin well to get all of it! Blitz briefly to break up the cornflakes and mix it all together.

If you don't have a blender, pop the cornflakes in a freezer bag and bash with a rolling pin, or a full water bottle, then tip the pieces into the coconut milk and leave to steep and infuse for 2 hours until very soft and soggy. Then combine with the condensed milk and carry on.

However you've arrived at your milky cornflake concoction, spoon it into an ice cube tray or two, and freeze for 2 hours.

Once frozen, pop the cubes out into a large mixing bowl and leave to thaw for 5 minutes. Cream together with a wooden spoon – this may take some effort, but persevere until it is thick and creamy. Then transfer the ice cream to a 400ml Tupperware or other freezer-safe container and return to the freezer.

TO KEEP: It will keep in the freezer for up to 4 months. Because of its simplicity, and the lack of a mechanical whisk or ice cream machine, this sets very firmly, so when you want to serve it, remove it from the freezer for 10 minutes to soften up, and mix well before serving.

PRUNE ICE CREAM

This was a hard sell in my household, and I'm sure you have your own feelings on it from the title alone, but let me tell you about it. Tinned prunes need a PR overhaul. You might associate them with an instant, er, 'digestive unblocker' from your childhood, and it's true that they are extremely effective at keeping the internal piping clear. But they're also utterly delicious, with a velvety texture that lends itself very well to soft-serve ice cream. Prunes and chocolate are a perfect pairing, but I've done that a lot in this book so far, so I wanted the prunes to stand proudly alone in this recipe. If you need some convincing, however, do feel free to add some smashed-up dark chocolate, or a couple of tablespoons of cocoa powder to this one. *(Pictured on previous page)*

SERVES 10

1 x 425g tin of prunes in juice or syrup

70g mixed nuts

5 eggs

100g finely ground sugar (plus 3 tbsp if using prunes in juice)

500ml double cream

Strain the prunes through a sieve set over a bowl to catch the juice or syrup – you'll be coming back for this later! De-stone the prunes by carefully squeezing each one at the sides and discard the stones. Roughly chop the prunes, then beat well with a fork to make them into a puree. Add a tablespoon of the juice or syrup to help them along the way, if you like. If you have a small bullet blender, you can throw them in and make this the work of a moment, but it's fairly quick to achieve by hand if you don't.

Next, line a 900g loaf tin, Tupperware box or empty ice-cream tub with two layers of cling film, using your fingers to push it into the corners and leaving a few centimetres spare all round. This is to make the ice cream easy to remove later. (If you don't have any cling film, you can skip this step, but it will get a bit messy at serving time.)

Gently heat a large non-stick pan and add the nuts, then pour over the reserved syrup and cook for 2–3 minutes until they start to stick together. If your prunes came in juice rather than syrup, add 3 tablespoons of finely ground sugar to kickstart the caramelization process, else you'll just end up with soggy nuts rather than sticky, delicious ones. Lightly grease a plate and tip out the nuts onto it to cool. Wash your pan immediately, as caramelized syrup can be extremely difficult to clean off once it has cooled down!

Separate the eggs, keeping the yolks and refrigerating the whites – you can make meringues with them or a simple egg-white omelette. Pop the yolks into a large mixing bowl and pour in the sugar. Add two-thirds of the prune mixture, and beat together until the yolks are pale and fluffy, or as pale and fluffy as they're going to be with some deep-purple prune pulp in there, and the mixture has doubled in size.

Add the cream and beat well until it forms soft peaks. If you have an electric whisk or stand mixer loitering around, now would be a great time to get it out, but if not, put some loud music on, get a rhythm going, and it'll be done before you know it.

When the mixture is light and fluffy and forms soft peaks – it should drop off an overturned spoon or your fingers slowly – you're good to go. Break up the caramelized nuts and scatter them over the bottom of the loaf tin, so that when turned out they will sit prettily on the top.

Carefully spoon the cream mixture into the tin. Give it a gentle shake to get it to settle into all the corners and smooth the top. Spoon in the remaining prune mixture and gently swirl it through with a knife to make a ripple effect. Carefully fold the cling film over the top and leave in the freezer for 4 hours or until frozen firm.

To serve, remove from the freezer, unwrap the cling film and turn out the ice cream onto a plate. Carefully peel away the cling film from the sides and base and leave for a few minutes at room temperature to soften before slicing.

TO KEEP: It will keep in the freezer for up to 4 months.

CHOCOLATE CHERRY CAKE

This recipe goes down a storm with a local cycling club, and I barely need the excuse to make it! Frozen cherries are cheaper and more convenient than fresh, as they come already de-stalked and pitted and can just be thrown in by the handful. I've used white chocolate in this iteration, but milk and dark work well too. Or try a combination, if you're feeling luxurious. If ground almonds are something you keep about the house then replace a third of the flour with some ground almonds for a Bakewell-esque taste sensation.

MAKES 9 GENEROUS PIECES

250g baking block
   or butter, plus extra
   for greasing
120g frozen or
   canned cherries
200g sugar
3 medium eggs
200g self-raising flour
100g white chocolate

TIP: *Exact measurements aren't necessary, but bear in mind that a slightly larger tin will cook faster as the traybake will be more shallow, and a slightly smaller one will take slightly longer as the batter will be more dense. If deviating from the size given here, adjust your timings to take it into account.*

Preheat the oven to 180°C/fan 160°C/350°F/gas 4 and ensure there is a shelf in the centre or just below it.

Lightly – and I mean very lightly, as this is a fat-rich cake so barely needs it – grease a 20 x 20cm cake tin or thereabouts.

If you're using frozen cherries and they're still, well, frozen, pop them into a microwave-proof bowl and zap them at full power for 90 seconds to defrost. Remove and stand to one side. (The cherries, that is, not you. Come back! Oh god, I'm turning into my dad already.)

Dice your butter into 2cm cubes and pop them into a large mixing bowl. Add the sugar and one of the eggs, and mash together with a fork to soften the butter, until you're able to beat it together into a sloppy buttercream consistency. Add the other two eggs and beat in well, then mix in the flour until well combined into a thick but smooth batter.

Roughly chop your chocolate into small chunks and tip into the batter along with the cherries. Fold in briskly, then scrape the whole lot into the prepared tin. Smooth the top with the back of your spoon, making sure the batter is pushed into all four corners, then place into the oven.

Bake in the centre of the oven for 50 minutes, or until a sharp knife inserted in the centre comes out clean. Remove and allow to cool in the tin for 10 minutes to firm up, before cutting into nine equally sized pieces (or unequally sized, depending on how much you want to share it!). Serve warm or cold.

TO KEEP: Leftovers (ha!) will keep in an airtight container or food storage bag for up to 3 days, or in the freezer for 3 months. Defrost and warm through to piping hot to serve for best results.

PBJ SANDWICH PUDDING

This twist on two classics is a favourite in my household, and the tin of custard may be an awful cheat, but goodness, it's a handy one. The only downside to this recipe – if indeed you can call it a downside at all – is that I usually have all of the component parts in my household at any given time, so I'm never more than half an hour away from this whenever it takes my fancy!

SERVES 6ISH

6 tbsp peanut butter
   (crunchy or smooth)
200ml whole milk
1 x 400g tin of custard
8 slices of white bread
4 tbsp red jam
butter, for greasing
frozen berries
1 tbsp sugar
salted peanuts, for
   topping (optional)

First make the peanut custard, by putting the peanut butter, milk and custard into a blender and blitzing it for a minute to combine everything. Set this to one side for a moment. If you don't have a blender, pop the peanut butter in the microwave for 30 seconds to melt it slightly, then scrape it into a large bowl. Add the milk, a little at a time, to loosen it, and then when the milk is all incorporated, add the custard and stir well until it's well combined.

Thickly spread each slice of bread on one side with the jam, then cut into quarters, squares or triangles – it all works out the same in the end.

Lightly grease a baking dish and place the jammy bread pieces in it, jam side up. Slowly pour over the peanut custard and press the bread down into it with your fingers. Scatter over the frozen berries as evenly as you can, then place the whole thing in the fridge or leave in a cool place for 30 minutes for the custard mixture to soak into the bread.

When the bread has absorbed some of the custard mixture and is looking all puffy and pleased with itself, turn your oven on to 180°C/fan 160°C/350°F/gas 4. Sprinkle some sugar and peanuts, if using, over the top of the pudding, and bake in the centre of the oven for 35 minutes.

Serve directly from the oven or reheat to piping hot to serve if made in advance.

TO KEEP: Leftovers will keep, covered well, in the fridge for 3 days, or in the freezer for 3 months. Defrost and reheat to piping hot throughout to serve.

CHOCOLATE ORANGE THUMBPRINTS

These small biscuits are an evolution from the very popular Peanut Butter and Jam Thumbprint Cookies in *A Girl Called Jack*, and are my go-to for birthdays, rainy days and the biscuit tin. Easy enough for the smallest of hands to help with, but decadent enough for the most grown up of palates.

MAKES 12 SMALL BISCUITS

50g baking spread or butter, plus a little extra to grease the baking sheet

2 tbsp sugar

2 tbsp cocoa powder

1 medium egg

8 tbsp self-raising flour

8 tsp orange marmalade

Preheat the oven to 180°C/fan 160°C/350°F/gas 4 and lightly grease a small baking tray or cookie sheet.

Weigh the baking spread into a mixing bowl and add your sugar and cocoa. Beat well with a fork or wooden spoon until well combined and even. Add the egg and mix again, taking care to incorporate it well into the mixture.

Add the flour, 2 tablespoons at a time, mixing well until it forms a soft, pliable dough. Take a walnut-sized piece and roll it into a ball to test its structural integrity. A little crumbling at the edges is to be expected, and indeed is part of the particular charm of this recipe, but any more than a little will need a very small splash of water added to the dough to bring it together. A teaspoon should suffice, if required.

With lightly floured or oiled hands, take a walnut-sized piece of dough and place it on your prepared baking tray. Flatten it twice with a fork, then repeat with the remaining dough. I weigh the entire lump of dough and divide it by 12, then weigh each individual piece to make sure they are even, but I am ridiculous, and this is by no means essential. (It is very satisfying, though!)

Repeat with the rest of the dough, and when you have used it all up, make a large dent in the centre of each biscuit with your thumb – and be bold about it; the larger the print, the more marmalade it holds!

Spoon a little marmalade into each indent – it will melt and spread out in the hot oven, so don't worry about being too neat about it.

Bake in the centre of the oven for 12 minutes, and allow to cool for 10 minutes to let the marmalade return to a non-volcanic temperature before tucking in!

TO KEEP: These will keep in an airtight container for 4 days, or in the freezer almost indefinitely, but they don't tend to stay around that long.

STICKY GINGER SYRUP CAKE

I have made several versions of this cake over the years, using golden syrup, treacle and maple syrup interchangeably, depending on what I had in my cupboard and budget at the time. I've added figs, sultanas, chopped mixed peel and dates on varying occasions, and used plain white sugar in some and dark brown sugar in others. It's extraordinarily versatile, and every single version of it has been received with delight and gusto by my friends and colleagues. This is the simplest and cheapest incarnation, which happens to also be my favourite. To make it vegan, simply replace the egg with 2 heaped tablespoons of marmalade or applesauce.

MAKES 12 SMALL STICKY SQUARES

100g baking spread, plus extra for greasing

200g sugar

1 large egg

100ml cold water or orange juice

75g fresh root ginger

1 tbsp baking powder

200g self-raising flour

a light pinch of salt

100ml golden syrup

Preheat the oven to 160°C/ fan 140°C/325°F/gas 3, and lightly grease a 22cm square tin, or one that's fairly similar in size.

If you have a small bullet blender, it would be really handy here for a smooth cake batter and even gingery taste, but if you don't, I'll talk you through making it without.

Cream together the baking spread and sugar in a large mixing bowl. Break in the egg and mix in with a fork until well combined. Add the water or orange juice a little at a time and beat well with a wooden spoon or spatula – I'll level with you, it's going to look horrendous, but stay with it, it gets better. Coarsely grate the ginger using the large holes on a box grater, and add to the general horror in the bowl – then think about buying a small bullet blender, so you never have to look at this again.

However you arrive at your soggy gingery conclusion, spoon in the baking powder and add the flour and salt, then mix well and briskly to form an even, lump-free batter. Pour it into the prepared tin and bake in the centre of the oven for 50–60 minutes, until risen and golden and a chopstick, toothpick or small sharp knife inserted into the centre comes away clean.

Remove from the oven and set on a wire cooling rack, if you have one, or a couple of small books if you don't. This allows the heat to escape from the base of the tin so you don't end up with a soggy bottom – but perhaps don't choose books that you're particularly precious about.

Pierce the cake around twenty times, top to bottom, with a chopstick or around fifty times with a cocktail stick. Pour over the syrup – I've estimated 100ml but you want a generous layer across the whole top of the cake. Leave it to stand for an hour so the syrup sinks through the whole cake, then slice and enjoy.

TO KEEP: Will keep in an airtight container for up to 4 days, or in the freezer for up to 6 months.

MICROWAVE PBJ BROWNIES

This microwave brownie is the ultimate in easy desserts, ready in less than 25 minutes and with hardly any washing up! They can be frozen and then defrosted thoroughly before eating. You could also add any fresh, frozen or tinned soft fruit, such as blueberries, raspberries or strawberries, or chocolate pieces to the brownies before cooking. As an alternative, you could make these blondies by removing the cocoa powder and replacing it with more flour. Omit the peanut butter if there is a nut allergy, of course; you can use tahini or sunflower seed butter as like-for-like replacements.

SERVES 6

75g unsalted or salted butter or soft baking spread, plus extra for greasing

50g peanut butter

100g dark chocolate

1 medium egg

50g plain flour

100g finely ground sugar, any kind

a few tsp red or purple jam (any flavour)

ice cream, cream or custard, to serve (optional)

First, lightly grease a 15cm microwaveable dish or bowl.

Add the butter, peanut butter and chocolate to another microwaveable bowl and cook, covered, on High for 30 seconds until melted. Remove from the microwave and stir thoroughly. Leave to cool slightly then add the egg and stir to combine. Tip the peanut butter mixture into the greased dish then sift in the flour and tip in the sugar. Mix gently to form a thick, sticky paste. Smooth the top of the mixture with a spoon.

Make holes in the top of the brownie mixture using a teaspoon and fill each generously with the jam. Place into the microwave and cook for 3–4 minutes on High. Remove and leave to cool for 15 minutes (it needs to rest to continue cooking). Serve on its own or with ice cream, cream or custard if desired.

TO KEEP: This will keep for up to 2 days covered in a cool, dark place. If you wanted to keep it nice and fudgy you could pierce the top with a fork and spread over 1 tablespoon of jam which will sink in and keep it moist.

BLACK FOREST MUG PUDDING

This pudding is quick and simple to rustle up, but tastes deliciously indulgent. You can use any red or purple jam, with or without 'bits' in it, for a tasty treat. Ideal for when you fancy a quick sweet something but don't want the bother of rustling up an entire cake!

SERVES 1

2 tbsp jam (any will do), plus extra for serving

2 tbsp chocolate spread, plus extra for serving

3 tbsp oil

3 tbsp milk

1 medium egg

2 tbsp honey or golden syrup

4 tbsp self-raising flour

Put the jam and chocolate spread into a mug and microwave for 30 seconds to soften. Stir in the oil and milk. Leave to cool for a minute or two.

Beat in the egg then mix in the honey or golden syrup. Stir in the flour, to make a smooth batter. Place the mug back in the microwave for 90 seconds on High. It will rise quite a bit, but it deflates again a little afterwards.

Top with a small dollop of jam and chocolate spread, then microwave for a few seconds until melted. Remove, and allow to stand for a minute or two before tucking in – as it will be hot.

TUPPENCE LEMONDROPS

These little melt-in-the-mouth biscuits are very, very moreish and very quick to pull together. Which is an incredibly dangerous combination, by all accounts. I hope you enjoy them as much as I do, and my friends and family do. . .

MAKES 16

150g lemon curd, plus extra for finishing

1 medium egg

150g self-raising flour, or 150g plain flour plus 2 tsp baking powder, plus extra for dusting

oil, for greasing

2 tbsp or 15g icing sugar (optional)

mini meringues (optional)

TIP: *The easiest way to cut your dough is to split it in half, then both the halves in half, then each of those in half, and so on and so forth until you have sixteen pieces of dough of roughly equal sizes.*

Preheat the oven to 170°C/ fan 150°C/325°F/gas 3 and make sure there is a shelf at the centre or just below it. I bake these cookies in two batches, but if you are going to do them all in one go, two shelves quite close to each other will do fine. Weigh your lemon curd into a mixing bowl and crack in the egg. Beat together with a fork until well combined; this takes some doing, as lemon curd can be unyielding.

Add the flour 2 tablespoons at a time and continue to beat in to form a smooth dough. Swap the fork out for a plastic or silicone spatula halfway through; this helps combine the ingredients more easily as the dough starts to stiffen.

Lightly flour your worktop, and your hands, and lightly grease a baking tray or two. I spray mine with spray oil, as it is swift and efficient.

Turn your dough out onto the lightly floured worktop and knead it swiftly to bring it together into a soft and pliable dough. Depending on the brand of lemon curd used – some are runnier or stickier than others – you may need to work in a little more flour. The dough should be soft but not stick to your hands.

Break your dough into sixteen evenly sized pieces (see Tip). Roll each knob of dough into a smooth ball and press it onto the baking tray with your thumb to flatten it out lightly. Leave a clear half inch around each cookie to allow for expansion.

Bake in the centre of the oven for 14 minutes precisely, then remove swiftly to cool. Dredge with icing sugar, if using, while hot. Finish with a mini meringue, if using, held in place with a tiny dollop of lemon curd, and allow to cool.

TO KEEP: The unbaked cookies may be frozen, flat, on a baking tray, then transferred to a freezer bag or container until ready to bake. Defrost on a baking tray for 4 hours at room temperature, then bake as instructed above. They will keep in an airtight jar or container for 5 days but are best eaten immediately after cooling.

MINCEMEAT BREAD PUDDING

Jars of mincemeat are often reduced after Christmas, or even in the run-up to it, as supermarkets look to clear their shelves of seasonal items and make way for the next promotional drive. I often pick up a few jars, as they are seriously good value for money for how much flavour you get, and here's one of my favourite uses for it. (The other is making miniature Eccles cakes or dolloping it into turmeric-stained rice to make a kind of fragrant sticky pilau to go with curries!) *(Pictured on next page)*

SERVES 4–6

300g bread

300ml whole milk, or leftover fruit juice from tinned fruits

50g baking spread, plus extra for greasing

300g mincemeat

1 medium egg

1 x 400g tin of custard, to serve (optional)

First dice your bread, tear it up or blast it in a food processor. They all give a similar result, with the food processor edging it for a slightly more even texture but not enough to justify yet more washing up, in my humble opinion. But do whatever feels right to you, with whatever you have at your disposal.

Place into a large mixing bowl that will easily hold twice its volume, and set aside for a moment.

In a second, smaller mixing bowl or jug, measure in the milk or the fruit juice, if using. Melt the spread and beat in quickly. Mix in the mincemeat – it won't look particularly pretty at this stage, but it all works itself out in a moment. Add the egg and beat in briskly with a fork, until the wet ingredients are well combined.

Pour the wet ingredients over the bread, and mix well. Leave to stand and absorb for 15 minutes.

Lightly grease a 450g loaf tin, 20cm cake tin (round or square), or individual pudding tins. Transfer the pudding mixture to the tin or divide it equally if using pudding tins.

Place in the centre of the oven at 190°C/fan 170°C/375°F/gas 5, covering with a little foil to prevent it from overly browning. You can remove this 10 minutes before the end if you like a crispy top and edge to your pudding. Bake for 50 minutes, checking with a knife, cocktail stick or skewer to the centre. It should be moist and dense but not underdone. If it clings to your implement, return it to the very bottom shelf of the oven for a further 10–15 minutes.

Serve with custard, or whatever suits.

TO KEEP: Leftovers will keep in the fridge, covered well or stored in an airtight container, for 3 days, or in the freezer for up to 6 months.

BITS AND PIECES ROCKY ROAD

This rocky road is a New Year's tradition in my household – a way of using up all of the leftover Christmas biscuits, chocolates, nuts and mixed fruit that's kicking around, and a nice gift for friends and family. 'One person's junk is another person's treasure' is very true in this scenario!

SERVES 10

130g butter, plus extra for greasing

200g any biscuits

3 tbsp honey or golden syrup

100g marshmallows

200g white or dark chocolate

15–20 Christmas chocolates

100g mixed dried fruit (optional)

100g any kind of nuts (optional)

icing sugar, for dusting

TIP: *Vegans can replace the butter with a vegan soft spread, and up the chocolate weight by 20% (because butter is firm at fridge temperature whereas vegan spreads tend not to be). All of the other ingredients can be easily substituted with vegan equivalents.*

First, grease and line a 20cm square baking tin (or a round one).

Pop your biscuits into a freezer bag and smash them to bits, either with a rolling pin, a full squash bottle or a can of beans. You want some chunky pieces, about the size of a 10p piece, and some sawdusty pieces.

Melt your butter in a non-stick pan on a low heat on the smallest hob ring, adding the honey or syrup and half of the marshmallows. Break up the chocolate and add that too, then melt everything together, stirring well.

Unwrap your Christmas chocolates and pop them in a mixing bowl while the pan does its thing. Add the dried fruit and nuts, if using, the biscuits, and the remaining marshmallows. Stir well to combine.

When the chocolate, butter, honey and marshmallow mixture is smooth and consistent, pour it over the biscuit mix. Stir well to coat everything lightly in the chocolate mixture, then transfer it all to your tin. Smooth the mixture into the corners of the tin and all the way to the sides, and press it down gently with the back of a spoon or your clean fingertips. Make sure to scrape as much of the mixture out of the bowl as you can!

Pop it in the fridge to set for 2 hours, then remove and slice into fingers or squares. Dust lightly with icing sugar, and enjoy.

TO KEEP: These will keep in the fridge for up to a week, but good luck keeping them around that long!

BAG OF TRICKS

My 'bag of tricks' is a collection of the day-to-day recipes and ideas
that I keep up my apron sleeves – from using up scrappy bits and pieces
to having some simple building blocks on hand that can be turned into
myriad different things. They're all fairly adaptable, so feel free to adjust
them according to what you have in or your own preferences, and make
them your own.

THE SUGAR HACK

You don't need to buy several kinds of sugar to keep in your store cupboard, even if you are the keenest of bakers. 'Granulated', 'caster', and 'icing' are not different varieties of sugar, but different grinds. If you have a small bullet blender, standard blender, food processor or mini chopper, you can get all three from one single bag of the cheapest granulated white stuff from the supermarket.

CASTER SUGAR

Simply decant however much you need from the bag of granulated sugar into the cup of your blender (or whatever implement you choose to use!) and pulse it for around 10 seconds to make caster sugar.

ICING SUGAR

For icing sugar, blitz it for around 30 seconds, dip a clean finger in to check how finely ground it is, and repeat if necessary.

EGG REPLACEMENTS

If you don't have any eggs to use in baking, try one of these instead. Some of these may not be to hand in your store cupboard, but I have included them because if you're anything like me, there's some dusty random ingredients knocking around in the hinterland of the top shelf that were bought for something forgettable and could do with being used up – I have included all of the options that I know of to be as helpful as possible, rather than a firm recommendation that you keep an avocado on hand 'just in case'!

TO REPLACE 1 MEDIUM EGG – SIMPLY MULTIPLY FOR LARGER BAKES

- 3 heaped tbsp applesauce
- 2 heaped tbsp marmalade, any kind
- 1 small ripe banana
- 50g soft tofu
- 3 tbsp natural yoghurt
- 2 tbsp aquafaba (the 'juice' from a can of chickpeas or white beans)

- 2 heaped tbsp peanut butter or other nut or seed butter
- 2 level tbsp cornflour, plus 2 tbsp warm water
- 1 tbsp of chia seeds, golden linseed or flax seeds, plus 3 tbsp cold water
- 1 tbsp light-coloured vinegar, plus 1 level tbsp baking powder
- ½ small ripe avocado

CHEAT-ROASTED GARLIC Ⓥ

Putting the oven on just to roast some garlic is certainly not in keeping with running a thrifty kitchen, although if you have it on for something else already I recommend popping a bulb or two on the bottom shelf for sticky-golden squishable cloves of loveliness. However, if you fancy this golden wonder in a hurry, here's a quick and simple shortcut.

MAKES 10–12 ROASTED CLOVES (DEPENDING ON THE SIZE OF YOUR BULB)

1 bulb of garlic
1 tsp light cooking oil

TIP: *If you find peeling the cloves hard work, chop the top and bottom off and drop them into a jug or bowl of boiling water. Allow to soak for a few minutes – they should slip right out of their skins.*

Simply break the bulb of garlic into cloves, and carefully rub away any excess papery skin with a clean tea towel. Pop the cloves into a microwave-safe bowl, and drizzle over the oil. Give it a gentle toss to very lightly coat the cloves in the oil, and then place it in the microwave.

Microwave on High for 20 seconds. Remove the dish carefully, shake gently, and repeat. Do not be tempted to do the full 40–60 seconds at once: the combination of hot oil and microwave energy can be an incredibly flammable one, so it's best to keep this in short bursts and your kitchen and hairline intact!

TO KEEP: You can squeeze out the cloves into a clean small jar with a lid and mix with a little oil to make a roasted garlic paste that will keep in the fridge for up to 1 week, or transfer them into a small ice-cube tray to keep for up to 3 months. You can fry them from frozen for convenience, too.

DIY LIGHT COOKING SPRAY (Ve)

'Light' cooking sprays aren't just for the calorie conscious, they're also efficient for lightly greasing baking sheets and cake tins, especially for butter-heavy bakes where you may not want to add any more to the equation. But they retail at an astronomical price relative to their actual ingredients, so one day I decided to try to make my own. Surely it was just an emulsification of oil and water? I flipped the bottle over and scanned the ingredients list. Sunflower oil, water and xanthan gum to stabilize it. Well, I wasn't making it to sit on a shelf or in a warehouse for a couple of years, so I left out the xanthan gum, and it worked just fine. I haven't bought a bottle of it since.

MAKES 1 X 190ML BOTTLE

You will need: a spray bottle – I use an old Frylight bottle, as it's ideal

120ml sunflower or vegetable oil
60ml cold water

First measure your oil into a clean, empty spray bottle, then add the water. Screw the lid onto the spray bottle tightly and shake vigorously for 30 seconds to combine and emulsify. It should come together to form a thin, creamy coloured liquid.

Spray the nozzle a couple of times to draw up the liquid so it's ready to use. Shake it well before each use in case it separates. Use five sprays to replace a tablespoon of oil when frying or roasting, and around ten sprays for a standard-sized cake tin or roasting dish ought to do the trick.

PORPOISE SEASONING Ⓥ

No porpoises were harmed in the creation of this recipe, it's just the daft name that I gave to my homemade all-purpose seasoning a while back and it's stuck! Use this to add layers of flavour to any fried or roasted meats or fish, soups, stews, casseroles, traybakes, roast potatoes, roasted vegetables and more.

MAKES ABOUT 200G

3 tbsp salt

4 tbsp sweet or smoked paprika

4 tbsp mixed dried herbs

1 tbsp ground black pepper

1 tbsp cumin, seeds or ground 3 tbsp sugar

1 tsp ground cinnamon

Simply measure all of the ingredients into a clean airtight jar, screw the lid on and shake well to combine. Label and store in a cool dry place.

TO KEEP: Store for up to 6 months.

SCRAPPY STOCK (Ve)

I keep a large, silicone, food-safe bag in the bottom drawer of my freezer, its mouth permanently open, for all of my veg peels and skins. When the bag is full, I make my 'scrappy stock'.

MAKES 1 LITRE OF STOCK

Veg to include liberally:

Onion, garlic, leek bottoms and tops, spring onion tops and bottoms, celery, carrot tops and peel, parsnip tops and peel, any herbs including stalks, fennel, sweet potato peel.

Veg to include sparingly:

Onion skins, potato peel or gouged-out eyes, the dark green tops of leeks, powdered or star anise, white pepper, carrot-top greens, mushroom stalks or whole mushrooms.

Sundries and supplements:

Salt, black pepper, mixed dried herbs, onion powder, garlic powder, bay leaves, celery leaves.

Best not to include:

Anything from the brassica family – like sprouts, cabbage, broccoli, cauliflower – as they can make the stock taste bitter.

Press down on your bag of veg scraps to squeeze the contents down as much as possible. Upend it into a large stock pot or a 3.5-litre slow cooker, along with enough water to cover, a hefty shake of mixed dried herbs and a few pinches of salt and pepper. Simmer over a low heat for 1.5–2 hours.

After the long simmer, pass the stock through a sieve or a colander to separate the veg from the liquid, pressing down firmly with a mug or other robust implement to extract as much of the stock as possible.

Return the strained stock to the pan on a rolling boil and cook until reduced down to just under a litre, before passing it through a second filter of kitchen roll lining a funnel, balanced on an old, but clean, recycled juice bottle. If your bottle is plastic, as many of them are, you should leave the stock to cool significantly before doing this stage, or else the bottle will warp and, in some cases, may split.

If the mixture is too heavily skewed towards onion skins, it may become bitter. I blanch these first in a separate pan, bringing the water to the boil first then dropping the onion peelings in, and then I pick out the skins and separate them from the onion layer. The skins get put onto the compost heap in the garden, and the onion flesh goes into the stockpot.

Use a good variety of vegetable bits to make a full-bodied and flavourful stock – you want at least as much of the good stuff, like carrot, parsnip, herb stalks and celery, as you have onions. It may help to store the onion separately to keep an eye on the levels of both, then use any extraneous for a rich onion soup or gravy, giviing it a quick blanch in a pan of boiling and very heavily salted water to remove the skins.

If your veg is particularly muddy, give it a quick blanch (as described above) to loosen any ingrained dirt, then drain and rinse thoroughly.

TO KEEP: Store it in a clean jar or bottle with a lid in the fridge for 4 weeks, or in a freezerproof container in the freezer for 6 months. If freezing, you may wish to pour the stock into an ice-cube tray.

SARDINE STOCK

Sardine stock is very common in traditional Chinese and Japanese cookery. I first came across it at a specialist Japanese food store in Shaftesbury Avenue, in Soho. The wrapper was bright green, so I picked it up thinking that it was vegetable stock, but really the picture of a big blue fish on the front should have been a bit of a giveaway. Nevertheless, I became obsessed with it and its deeply savoury base notes that complement a wide variety of dishes. Ramen, risotto, pasta sauces, hot and sour soup, creamy mushroom soups – the possibilities are almost limitless. And so, in that mischievous and tinkering tendency that I revel in, and to save myself a four-hour return trip when I ran out, I eventually levelled up to making my own. I'll be honest with you, the house smelled fairly ripe for a day or so, so you might want to open the kitchen window before cracking on with this one.

MAKES 500ML OF STRONG STOCK

1 large onion
2 large carrots
4 celery stalks
1 tsp salt
plenty of black pepper
1 litre cold water
2 x 120g tins of sardines in olive or sunflower oil
a dash of bottled lemon juice

TIP: Don't throw away the very soft fish and veg pieces when you have strained your stock – you can combine these with instant mash (or the regular kind and a little flour) to make fishcakes!

First peel and finely slice the onion, then wash and finely slice the carrots and celery. Finely slicing your veg reveals more of the surface area, which imparts more flavour into the broth and also cuts down the cooking time. Pop all the chopped veg into a saucepan, along with the salt and pepper, and cover with the cold water.

Add the sardines, including the oil, which will add a richness to your final stock. Bring to the boil, then reduce to a simmer and cook for around 30 minutes. If you have a slow cooker, you can put the whole lot into it and cook on a high heat for 2 hours, then reduce to low for a further 6 hours or overnight. (If you do it this way, use only 600ml of water as it won't reduce in the same way as it would on the boil.)

However you achieve your stock, strain it through a sieve or colander lined with kitchen roll to catch all of the little crumbly bits of bone (see Tip), then return the liquid to the hob in a clean pan and reduce it further until it will fit in a clean jar with a lid.

TO KEEP: Store it in a clean jar or bottle with a lid in the fridge for 4 weeks, or in a freezerproof container in the freezer for 6 months. If freezing, you may wish to freeze it in an ice-cube tray for easily accessible portions if you aren't going to use it all at once.

CRAB STOCK

Crab stock is excellent for making soups, risottos, quick and easy tomato pasta dishes, or as the base for spicy noodles. It does feel a little cheeky calling this a recipe at all, but it is something I make fairly often, and it's a handy thing to have up your sleeve if you fancy something that tastes like a restaurant dinner but that can be made on an extremely tight budget.

MAKES 500ML OF STRONG STOCK

1 large onion

2 medium carrots

4 celery stalks

plenty of black pepper

1 chicken, fish or vegetable stock cube

1 litre cold water

1 x 75g jar of crab paste

a dash of bottled lemon juice

First peel and finely slice your onion, then wash and finely slice the carrots and celery. Finely slicing your veg reveals more of the surface area, which imparts more flavour into the broth and also cuts down the cooking time. Pop the veg into a saucepan, along with the pepper, crumble in the stock cube and cover with the cold water. Bring to the boil.

Scrape your crab paste into a mug and add a few tablespoons of the boiling stock from the pan. Stir well with a fork to loosen it into a smoother paste, then repeat with a little more boiling water. Repeat until the mug is two-thirds full and there are no lumps in the crabby liquid. Pour the liquid from the mug into the saucepan and stir well.

Simmer for around 30 minutes, or transfer the whole lot to a slow cooker for 2 hours on High and then 6 hours on Low to extract all of the flavour from the veg.

If you have a blender, transfer the stock to it and blend until smooth. If you don't have a blender, simply strain out the veg and reduce the stock to fit into a clean jam jar with a lid or similar.

TO KEEP: Store in a clean jar or bottle with a lid in the fridge for 4 weeks, or in a freezerproof container in the freezer for 6 months. If freezing, you may wish to freeze it in an ice-cube tray for easily accessible portions if you aren't going to use it all at once.

CHICKEN STOCK

I was very tempted to write a glib 'don't bother; I use stock cubes and so does almost everyone else that I know', but this recipe for chicken stock is not a religious espousement that Only Real Chicken Stock Is Good Enough, rather an idea for what to do should you find yourself with a surfeit of bones and scraps, such as from chicken wings, drums and thighs, or a whole chicken. When I make thighs or drums for a crowd, I have absolutely no shame about handing everyone a knife to tackle their chicken with, so I can pilfer the bones and scraps for stock from their plates; it's one of the only circumstances around my table where I am a stickler for cutlery! This is a good place to use soft bendy carrots, drying onions or anything else that's past its best for everyday cooking.

MAKES 500ML OF STRONG STOCK

2 onions
6 fat cloves of garlic
2 large carrots
4 celery stalks
chicken bones and scraps
2 tsp mixed dried herbs
1 tsp salt
plenty of black pepper
1 litre cold water

First peel and slice your onions, then peel the garlic cloves and halve them lengthways. Chop the carrots and celery and pop all the veg into a large saucepan. Add the chicken bones and scraps, herbs, salt and pepper, then pour over the cold water and bring to the boil. Once you've reached a rolling boil, reduce the heat to a vigorous simmer, cover the pan with a lid, and leave bubbling away for 30 minutes.

Remove from the heat and leave to cool and continue to cook in its own flavourful juices for a further hour. This continues to extract the flavours and enrich the stock, without the need to keep your gas or electricity bill ramping up in the background!

Strain the infused stock to remove the chicken bones and veg. Pick out the bones and discard them – you can keep the meat and veg as the base for a chicken pie or pasta dish; it will be very soft and tender and full of flavour!

Return the strained stock to a clean pan and boil vigorously to reduce it to fit into a clean jam jar with a lid, or similar.

TO KEEP: Store in a clean jar or bottle with a lid in the fridge for 4 weeks, or in a freezerproof container in the freezer for 6 months. If freezing, you may wish to freeze it in an ice-cube tray for easily accessible portions if you aren't going to use it all at once.

TIP: You can also make a chicken-style vegetable stock by adding plenty of carrot and celery to the base of my Scrappy Stock (see page 218), and a couple of sheets of gelatine or vege-gel according to the packet instructions, to replicate the glutinous mouthfeel of authentic chicken stock.

MUSHROOM STOCK (Ve)

A fine substitute for beef stock, or as a rich umami flavour in its own right, just a dash of this dark, treacle-hued and pungent liquid is enough to enrich and enliven any savoury dish in need of a little help in the flavour department. Use it as a risotto base, for mushroom soups, lasagne, ragus, Bolognese, as a ramen stock, to add depth to a casserole or lentil dishes – the possibilities are almost endless.

MAKES 500ML OF STRONG STOCK

1 large onion or 1 leek
6 cloves of garlic
400g mixed mushrooms
2 litres cold water
2 tbsp dark soy sauce
½ tsp mixed dried herbs (optional)
plenty of salt and black pepper

First peel and chop your onion or leek and pop it into a large saucepan. Peel the garlic and halve it lengthways to expose more of the surface area, then add it to the pan. Halve your mushrooms and add those too. Cover with the cold water, then add the soy sauce, herbs and plenty of salt and pepper.

Bring the pan to the boil, then reduce the heat and simmer vigorously for around 30 minutes, then remove from the heat and allow to infuse for a further 2 hours. Strain through a sieve into a bowl – you can keep the veg to use in a pasta sauce, casserole or pie filling – and boil the strained liquid until it reduces down to around 500ml.

TO KEEP: Store in the fridge in a clean jar or bottle with a lid for up to 2 weeks, or in the freezer for up to 6 months. If freezing, you may wish to freeze it in an ice-cube tray for easily accessible portions if you aren't going to use it all at once.

ODDS AND SODS GRAVY

I sometimes make this gravy from the outer skins of onions that I stash in the freezer, and sometimes I make it from whole ones, depending on what I have kicking around. The onions give it a rich, sweet base that makes it suitable for all manner of roast dinners – and the cranberry sauce is a delicious, although not entirely essential, addition.

SERVES 4

2 large onions

3 chicken or vegetable stock cubes

2 tbsp or 35g cranberry sauce (optional – don't buy it especially!)

2 tbsp or 30g flour

3 tbsp light cooking oil or 40g soft spread

a pinch of mixed dried herbs

300ml cold water

First peel your onions, quarter them, and pop them into a small powerful blender along with all the other ingredients, including the cold water. Blend until completely smooth.

Pour into a heavy-based saucepan and bring to the boil, then reduce to a simmer and cook slowly and gently for around 40 minutes, stirring every now and then. If you have a small slow cooker this is perfect to put in the night before and set on Low, then wake up the next morning to the smell of gravy wafting through the house!

Thin to your desired consistency with extra water – if this is for a roast dinner then any of the water from cooking the roast potatoes is ideal as it's starchy and warm and salty, and this way it also doesn't go to waste!

You can let the gravy cool and then microwave it when you need it, or heat it through on the hob to serve, but it does thicken as it cools so if you plan to do that, make it a bit thinner than you'd like to serve it.

TO KEEP: Will keep in the fridge for 2 days, but it will thicken so thin with a bit more boiling water before serving.

TIP: *I have an alcohol-free house, but if you have some cheap red or white wine or even cider kicking about, a splash or two of it in this gravy would be delicious! You can also add the fat and juices that seep out from cooking any meats or sausages, to really give it a rich and succulent flavour. If you're planning to do this, maybe dial down the oil or soft buttery spread a bit!*

BASIC SALAD DRESSING (Ve)

Knowing the formula for a basic salad dressing is a skill that, once memorized, will serve you well for using up whatever you have to hand. The possibilities and combinations are endless, but it starts with a little maths and science to get you going. The ideal dressing is a carefully balanced combination of fat, acid, salt and heat – usually a light oil, lemon or vinegar, salt and pepper, mustard or chilli.

MAKES AROUND 180ML, OR 12 X 1 TBSP SERVINGS

7 tbsp light cooking oil
5 tbsp light-coloured vinegar or lemon juice
a few pinches of salt
a generous grind of black pepper

First measure your oil into a medium-sized clean jar with a tight-fitting lid. Add the vinegar or lemon juice and the salt and pepper. Screw the lid on tight and shake well to combine and emulsify; the dressing should transform from a translucent liquid to a creamy-coloured one as the fats and acids combine.

TO KEEP: Store it in the fridge for up to 2 weeks, giving it a little shake before using each time.

ENGLISH DRESSING (Ve)

A twist on the classic French dressing, but using English mustard, as it tends to be cheaper in the larger supermarkets. A fiery challenge to its sophisticated muse, and useful for all manner of dishes – from pepping up a mild bean salad or warm baby potatoes, to adding a little last-minute vigour to hot cooked dishes like curries and casseroles.

MAKES AROUND 120ML, OR 8 X 1 TBSP SERVINGS

1 tsp English mustard
2 tbsp light-coloured vinegar
a pinch of sugar
a pinch of salt
6 tbsp light cooking oil

Spoon the English mustard into a small bowl, and add the vinegar. Whisk the two together with a fork to combine thoroughly for a minute. Add your sugar and salt and whisk briskly, then add the oil a tablespoon at a time, beating with the tines of the fork continuously until well combined.

TO KEEP: Store in the fridge in a small bottle or jar, thoroughly cleaned with an airtight lid, for up to 2 weeks. Shake well before using.

TINNED FRUIT JUICE DRESSING Ⓥⓔ

I'm yet to come across a fruit juice that doesn't work as a salad dressing in some format, although you may want to tinker with the flavours to see what takes your fancy, or adjust them according to what you have in your cupboard. I've given some suggestions below to get you started, but the possibilities and variations are as limitless as your imagination. Scale up or down the quantities depending on what you manage to squeeze out of your tin. You can use ordinary fresh fruit juice as well, and the 'from concentrate' variety is also absolutely fine. I'd draw the line at squash or smoothies, personally, but other than that, pretty much anything goes. Don't chuck away the drained-off fruit juice when you are using a tin of fruit, this is a perfect way to use every last bit.

MAKES 250ML

100ml fruit juice
75ml light cooking oil
75ml light-coloured
   vinegar
¼ tsp salt
plenty of black pepper

Measure all of your ingredients into a large, very clean jar or bottle with a tight-fitting lid. Seal it well and shake vigorously for 30 seconds until well combined. Store in the fridge.

TO KEEP: Store in the fridge in a small bottle or jar, thoroughly cleaned with an airtight lid, for up to 3 weeks. Shake well before using.

TIP: *Some additional ingredients you might like to consider, depending on which fruit juice you have to hand:*

Chilli flakes or a whole small red one, pierced all over with a fine pin, goes well with both mandarin juice and pineapple juice.

Fresh basil, or the finely chopped stalks, is a welcome addition to grapefruit, melon and mandarin juice. This particular dressing won't last as long due to the fresh greenery, so either strain it back out after a few days and re-jar it for up to 2 weeks, or use within a week of making.

A dash of any kind of mustard is delicious in a pear juice dressing, as is a rind of strong cheese, or blue cheese, or a piece that has hardened in the fridge.

Fresh rosemary, stalks and all, goes well with a mandarin juice dressing for a Greek vibe.

Whole or lightly bashed-up garlic cloves are a welcome companion for any and all salad dressings. They will turn a bit of a grim colour after a few days – this is totally normal.

Balsamic vinegar goes well with pear juice and prune juice, but it is sweeter than lighter vinegars, so add half of each to balance the acidity. You may need a little extra vinegar with the prune juice, as some brands can be quite syrupy.

TINNED FRUIT JUICE OR SYRUP

As well as salad dressings, you can reserve the fruit juice or syrup from tinned or preserved fruits and use them in all manner of ways. I tend to fling them all in a clean, large jar or bottle together in the fridge (one for juice, one for syrup) to make a 'fruit cocktail' flavour that's incredibly versatile.

FOR THE JUICE

- Use it in a salad dressing, as on the opposite page, or as the basis for a meat marinade for roasting, frying or barbecuing. Simply add a little oil and vinegar, and some herbs and spices: mixed dried herbs and chilli are a classic combination that works to complement the sweetness of mandarin juice, pear, prune, pineapple, and any others you can think of.

- Or simply dilute it with water or lemonade and some ice to enjoy as a refreshing drink.

- Use to soak dried fruit in for a few hours to fold into fruit breads, bread puddings, scones or sponge cakes.

- Mix with icing sugar in place of water to make a fruit-flavoured icing, ideal for pepping up plain biscuits or drizzling over a simple sponge cake.

FOR THE SYRUP

- Use it to moisten and refresh tired sponge cakes, by gently prodding some holes in the cake with a skewer or cocktail stick, and slowly and evenly pouring the syrup over the top. Leave it to soak in and reinvigorate it, and enjoy it as a sticky sweet snack.

- Reduce it in a small pan on the hob to make a thicker syrup, and pour over plain ice cream or pancakes.

- Soak old white bread in it and use as the basis for a simple bread pudding. Simply cut the soaked bread into triangles and arrange them in a lightly greased baking dish, pour a tin of custard over the top, and bake at 160°C/fan 140°C/325°F/gas 3 in the centre of the oven for around 30 minutes or until golden and caramelizing at the edges.

HERBSTALK OIL (Ve)

If you do buy or grow fresh herbs, pop them in a clean jar with a finger's-width of water in the bottom of it, and slip them into the fridge door to keep them fresher for longer. When, however, they are beyond redemption and either a little crispy or a little soggy around the edges, it's time to turn them into something else. This bright green, herb-flavoured oil is ideal for dressing a salad, marinating meat, chicken or mushrooms, adding to a soup to enliven it a little, or tossing liberally over a tin of mixed beans or cooked potatoes for an instant lunch.

MAKES 100ML

a fistful of soft herbs and their stalks, e.g. basil, flat leaf parsley, coriander, curly leaf parsley, mint

100ml light cooking oil

2 tbsp light-coloured vinegar

2 tbsp fresh water

a few pinches of salt

Throw everything into the small cup of a small bullet blender and whizz to a smooth green liquid. Pour it into ice-cube trays to freeze in handy portions (the water and vinegar help the freezing process as oil doesn't freeze very well!) or pour it into a small sterilized jar in the fridge and use within 4 weeks. Shake it every now and then to redistribute; discoloration is normal but if it goes brown and sludgy, throw it away!

No blender? No problem! Simply chop the herbs and stalks up very finely with a large sharp knife, then sprinkle the salt over them and chop again. The salt granules help to 'rough up' the leaves, meaning they will break down more easily. Transfer them to your small clean jar, and add the oil, vinegar and water. Screw the lid on tightly and shake well to combine. The three clear liquids will end up as a milky-looking opaque one; that's called emulsification and still slightly blows my mind every time I do it. And my 12-year-old son's, who has had many an impromptu science lesson off the back of a salad dressing.

TO KEEP: If storing in the fridge, use it within 4 weeks. If storing in the freezer, use it within 6 months.

BASIC MEAT MARINADES

A typical meat marinade is made up of four component parts: salt, fat, acid and flavour. The salt is fairly self-explanatory. The fat is usually one that is liquid at fridge temperature, because that's where longer marinades tend to take place for food safety reasons, so a sunflower oil would be fine. For acid, you want a lemon juice or vinegar, as this will help to tenderize and break down the fibres of the meat, but tomato juice and pineapple juice also work well. And for flavour; anything goes. Here are a few of my favourite combinations, given in quantities that will marinate around 200g of meat or fish.

WHITE FISH:	CHICKEN:	PORK BELLY:	SAUSAGES (SKIN PIERCED ALL OVER WITH A FORK):	CHICKEN LIVERS:
1 tbsp soy sauce	Pinch of salt	1 tbsp soy sauce	Pinch of salt	Pinch of salt
+	+	+	+	+
3 tbsp sunflower oil	3 tbsp sunflower oil	3 tbsp sunflower oil	1 tbsp oil	2 tbsp oil
+	+	+	+	+
1 tbsp light-coloured vinegar	1 tbsp lemon juice	1 tbsp orange juice or marmalade	1 tbsp light-coloured vinegar	1 tbsp red wine vinegar
+	+	+	+	+
fresh grated root ginger	1 tsp mixed dried herbs	plenty of black pepper	1 tbsp marmalade	1 tsp mixed dried herbs
	+		+	+
	plenty of black pepper		¼ tsp English mustard	plenty of black pepper

SOFFRITTO PASTE (Ve)

You can buy little jars of soffritto paste from the speciality cooking ingredients section of most large supermarkets, but it's extremely easy and far more economical to make your own. This jar of soothingly creamy yellow paste contains nothing more exotic than a triumvirate of celery, carrots and onions, with a little oil, salt and pepper. I make mine and freeze it in ice-cube trays, then when frozen, transfer them to a freezer bag to save storage space – and to free up the ice-cube trays for something else! If your cubes are small, you can use them from frozen, simply add to a warm pan with a splash of light cooking oil and stir as they start to melt, then go from there.

MAKES AROUND 800G, DEPENDING ON THE SIZE OF YOUR VEG

2 large carrots

2 large onions

6 cloves of garlic

4 large, full celery stalks or 6–8 pre-trimmed stalks

50ml light cooking oil

½ tsp salt

a good grind or pinch of black pepper

1 tbsp lemon juice or light-coloured vinegar

Wash your carrots but don't peel them. Finely slice them and set to one side for a moment. Peel and slice the onions and garlic, and chop the celery.

Warm the oil in a large non-stick pan, and add your carrots, onion, garlic and celery. Season with the salt and pepper. Cook on a gentle heat for around 20 minutes to soften, stirring occasionally so the veg doesn't catch and burn on the pan.

When the onions are translucent and the carrots and celery are soft, transfer everything to a blender, including any oils and juices from the pan. Pulse a few times to form a rough paste; you may need to add a splash of water depending how powerful your blender is.

And voilà, you have soffritto paste.

TO KEEP: Portion it into small jars (like the jars from spices) and freeze until required. Will keep in the fridge for 3 days in a clean lidded jar or food storage bag, or in the freezer for 6 months.

TIP: *You can use this as the base for dozens of different recipes – from risottos to soups, stews and pasta sauces. Add a chicken stock cube, some coconut milk and curry powder and blend to make an almost-instant soup. Stir this through hot pasta with plenty of cheese and black pepper. Spread it on toast and top with cheese and pop it under the grill. Add to a pan with rice, stock and cheese to make a risotto. Add it to cooked soft red lentils with curry powder for a quick and easy something-like-a-tarka-dal (but not quite!).*

STARTING BLOCKS (Ve)

I call these 'starting blocks' because they are useful for kickstarting many, many different recipes – soups, stews, curries, casseroles, hearty pasta sauces. Just pop a couple out of the freezer as and when required to save yourself a bit of chopping and prep. This is an ideal use for the 'top layer' and ends of onions if you've been saving them in the freezer for stock, as well as the tops and ends of leeks and spring onions.

MAKES AROUND 30 BLOCKS

2 large onions

1 large carrot

½ head of celery

1 whole bulb of garlic

½ tsp salt

2 tbsp light cooking oil

handful of parsley (stalks are fine)

plenty of black pepper

Peel and slice or chop your onions and slice the carrots and celery. Peel the garlic cloves. Pop everything into a small bullet blender, along with the salt, oil, parsley stalks and plenty of black pepper. Add a splash of water and blend everything together to a thick paste – you may need to add a little more water to get it going.

When everything is blended together, spoon it into an ice-cube tray or two and freeze for 2–4 hours.

When frozen, pop the cubes out into a food-safe bag or container, and return to the freezer, freeing up your ice-cube trays for something else!

You can use these blocks from frozen; simply add a few to a hot non-stick pan with a little oil and stir to melt them.

FIRESTARTER BLOCKS Ⓥⓔ

Similar to the 'starting blocks' on the previous page, but with a little bit of vigour, these are ideal to keep on hand for curries of all persuasions, feisty soups and anything you fancy imparting a little heat into.

MAKES AROUND 30 BLOCKS

2 large onions
50g fresh root ginger
1 whole head of garlic
4–6 small red or green chillies, or 2 tsp chilli flakes or powder
1 tsp salt
2 tbsp light cooking oil
plenty of black pepper

First peel and finely slice your onions, then slice the ginger. Peel the garlic and cut the stalks off the chillies if you're using fresh ones. Put everything into a small bullet blender, along with the salt, oil and plenty of pepper.

Add a splash of water and blend everything together to a thick paste – you may need to add a little more water to get it going.

When everything is blended together, transfer it to an ice-cube tray or two, and freeze for 2–4 hours.

When frozen, pop the cubes out into a food-safe bag or container, and return to the freezer, freeing up your ice-cube trays for something else!

You can use these from frozen; simply add a few to a hot non-stick pan with a little oil and stir to melt them.

BANANA PEEL CHILLI KETCHUP (Ve)

This nifty little use for banana skins is an ideal accompaniment to a curry, slathered on grilled cheese, dolloped on the side of a pile of mac 'n' cheese, spread on toast, crackers, or eaten as a dip with vegetables or cheesy nachos – it's extremely versatile! And once you've got the measure of it, you can adjust it to taste – add more heat by upping the mustard and chilli, make it a little more sour with extra vinegar, or pad it out by adding a hefty amount of sweet softened onion to the base.

MAKES 1 LARGE JAR

4 bananas, peel and all
1 large onion
4 fat cloves of garlic
100g sugar
100ml light-coloured vinegar
½ tsp chilli powder
1 tbsp mustard (any works)

Peel the bananas and break the chunks into a bowl, then mash them with a fork until well broken up and a bit sloppy. Very finely slice the peel, discarding only the tough stalk at the top and the puckered end, and transfer to a medium-sized saucepan, preferably a non-stick one or one with a heavy bottom. Peel and finely slice the onion and garlic cloves and add them to the pan, along with the sugar, vinegar, chilli and mustard.

Turn the heat up to medium and cook for a few minutes, stirring intermittently, then add the banana chunks and peel. Turn the heat down a fraction and cook for a few minutes until the banana mixture starts to bubble and spit at you.

Reduce the heat to low and cook for 30 minutes, or until the liquid has reduced by a third and thickened. Remove from the heat and pour into a clean, sterilized jar (see page 90 on how to sterilize jars).

Seal and leave to cool before transferring to the fridge.

If you would prefer a smoother ketchup, you can blend the peel and flesh together in a small bullet blender at the start, along with the garlic, sugar, mustard, chilli and vinegar, and cook it all on a low, slow heat for around 30 minutes, stirring intermittently so it doesn't catch and burn. When I've done it this way the ketchup ends up a darker yellow, and sometimes a ruddy brown, so I add a dash of turmeric to pep it back up again and make it look bright and appetizing. Both methods are equally as good – the chunky version is great in cheese sandwiches, whereas the smoother version is easier to smuggle past suspicious palates.

TO KEEP: Will keep in the fridge in clean, airtight jar for 3 months – it may darken in colour, but that's totally normal.

NOMATO SAUCE (Ve)

This sauce is handy to have on standby for guests who are sensitive to tomatoes; for a while back in 2019 I had to omit them from my diet while I underwent allergy testing, and in doing so I discovered an entire community of people online who had to avoid tomatoes in their diets for various reasons. I set about trying to make an affordable replica for tinned tomatoes and passata – I tend to try to deal with tricky situations by looking for the opportunity in them, and although I can now happily enjoy tomatoes again, I know that this recipe has been very useful for an often-overlooked core of my readership, so I'm including it here.

MAKES 2 DECENT-SIZED JARS

320g onion, or 2
    medium-sized ones
320g carrots, or
    2 large ones
200g red, orange or
    yellow peppers,
    or mixed frozen
4 fat cloves of garlic
2 tbsp light cooking oil
a pinch of salt
1 tsp light-coloured
    vinegar
2 tsp mixed dried herbs
a pinch or grind of
    black pepper

TIP: There's no need to peel the carrots here. A lot of the fibre and essential nutrients are contained in and under the skin.

First peel and slice your onion, then wash and slice your carrot.

Carefully cut out the stalk from the peppers if using fresh ones, using a small sharp knife and going in from the top so you lose as little of the actual pepper flesh as possible.

Peel the garlic, and put the onion, carrots, peppers and garlic into a blender, along with the cooking oil, salt, vinegar, herbs and pepper. Add enough water to come halfway up the vegetables, and blend to a paste.

When the veg is all blended together, decant it into a saucepan and cook gently for around 20 minutes on a medium heat, adding a little more water if needed to loosen it as it cooks.

Remove from the heat and divide into clean jars, leaving about half an inch of room in the neck of the jar if freezing. Screw the lids on tightly, label the jars, and allow them to cool at room temperature before storing for future use.

TO KEEP: Will keep in the fridge in clean, airtight jars or containers for 4 days, or in the freezer for up to 6 months. Defrost thoroughly in the fridge overnight and reheat to piping hot to serve.

TOMATO SAUCE Ⓥⓔ

A basic tomato sauce is an essential standby for quick pasta dinners, casseroles and more. I opt for tinned plum tomatoes over the chopped variety because, gram for gram, they tend to be identically priced but you get more tomatoes in the plum than in the chopped, which tend to be a little more watery. And the plum tomatoes generally have a richer flavour and colour, too, making them far better value for money. It's a small difference, but over time it really adds up!

MAKES 2 DECENT-SIZED JARS

2 x 400g tins of plum tomatoes

2 tbsp sunflower oil

2 tbsp light-coloured vinegar

a generous pinch of salt

1 tbsp mixed dried herbs

1 tbsp sugar

plenty of black pepper

Pour the tomatoes and their juice into a large saucepan, and refill one of the tins with cold tap water and add that too. Add the oil, vinegar, salt, herbs, sugar and plenty of black pepper.

Bring to a simmer – not to the boil – and mash the plum tomatoes with either a masher, a fork or a sturdy wooden spoon or spatula to break them down.

Simmer everything together for around 20 minutes, until the sauce is reduced by around a third and is thick and glossy. Transfer to two clean jars to store until needed.

TO KEEP: Will keep in the fridge in clean, airtight jars or containers for 4 days, or in the freezer for up to 6 months.

CHIP SHOP CURRY SAUCE

One of my very first jobs was working at the local fish and chip shop (see opposite). This recipe is not, alas, the secret recipe from there, but it's as close as I have managed to make it to the curry sauce that I remember. The wall-mounted urn and styrofoam cups are, of course, optional, but keeping a jar of this in my kitchen for impromptu pickled-egg snacks is entirely mandatory.

MAKES A DECENT-SIZED JAR

2 chicken or vegetable stock cubes

6 tbsp plain flour

6 tbsp medium curry powder

2 tbsp turmeric

2 tbsp sugar

a pinch of salt

a splash of light cooking oil, such as sunflower oil (optional)

Crumble the stock cubes well into a bowl, and add the flour, curry powder, turmeric, sugar and salt. Mix well with a fork to combine everything evenly, ensuring that the stock cubes are completely broken down. Store in an airtight, clean jar until required.

To make, boil the kettle and spoon 2 heaped tablespoons into a mug or jug. Add a splash of boiling water, and mix well with a fork to form a paste, then continue to add more boiling water, a little at a time, until it forms your desired consistency. I sometimes like to add a splash of light cooking oil to give it a richer texture, but this is entirely optional.

TO KEEP: The dry mixture will keep indefinitely in a clean jar, stored in a cool place out of direct sunlight.

AN EXTRA HELPING

In my early teens, I worked at the local fish and chip shop a short walk from my parents' house. The manager was an 'Uncle', George, in the way that I later came to learn that almost all of the Greek-Cypriot people who lived in Southend were not actually aunties or uncles in the familial sense, but friends of my grandad; the moniker used to denote a term of mutual respect rather than an endless network of blood bonds.

Before I was allowed anywhere near the vast rolling depths of boiling hot oil, I was taught to do all of the supplementary jobs that kept the shop stocked for our many loyal customers, and one of my favourites was to make the curry sauce to order. A few tablespoons of a mystery powder were decanted into a styrofoam cup, filled a third of the way with boiling water from a wall-mounted urn, stirred with a wooden chip fork, then slowly thinned out with more water until the cup was almost full.

I asked George several times what was in the mystery powder, and he would tap his nose and reply 'George's secrets' with an impish grin. I can honestly say I loved working there, for all the regulars with their same-as-always orders, the alchemy of watching sloppy batter turn to something crisp and delicious in a matter of seconds in his vast, calloused and heavily burned hands, the 'scraps' that we would stuff into thickly buttered bread rolls, the two ten-pound notes I would be handed with a flourish at the end of the week, and the distinctive booming laughter of the proprietor when he was in a good mood, which was pretty much his permanent state.

BASIC MILD CURRY SAUCE (Ve)

This recipe is different to the chip shop curry sauce; it's based on the Smartprice jar at Asda that I used to keep on standby in the cupboard for a busy day. It makes for a quick and easy dinner on the fly, and can be used with chicken, chickpeas, mushrooms, sausages – pretty much anything you fancy. The mild flavour makes it an ideal introductory 'curry' for young children or fussy palates, too.

MAKES 2 DECENT-SIZED JARS

1 large onion

4 fat cloves of garlic

20g fresh root ginger

1 x 400g tin of plum tomatoes

1 x 400g tin of coconut milk

2 tbsp medium curry powder

4 tbsp dried sultanas

1 tbsp ground turmeric

4 tbsp sunflower oil

a generous pinch of salt

plenty of black pepper

First, peel and slice your onion and peel your garlic, and transfer to a blender.

Add the ginger, tinned tomatoes and their juice, coconut milk, curry powder, sultanas, turmeric and sunflower oil, along with a generous pinch of salt and plenty of black pepper. Blend everything together to a smooth sauce.

Pour the sauce into a saucepan, and simmer everything together on a medium heat for around 20 minutes, stirring occasionally so it doesn't stick and burn at the bottom of the pan. Taste it and add more curry powder if you'd like to.

When the sauce has thickened and lost the acerbic raw edge from the onions, divide it between two clean jars, leaving around half an inch of space at the top if freezing. Screw the lids on tightly, label the jars, and leave them to cool completely at room temperature for a couple of hours.

TO KEEP: Will keep in the fridge for 4 days, or the freezer for 6 months. Defrost completely in the fridge overnight and reheat to piping hot to serve.

GARLIC JAM Ⓥⓔ

This started out, as so many of my recipes do, as a curious thought in the back of my head, then turned into an impulse, an obsession, an experiment and an evangelical triumph. I knew that garlic softened and sweetened with a long, slow cook, so I wondered if it would work as a slightly savoury, hint-of-caramel condiment? I scribbled some notes based on what little I knew about jam-making, dug out an old onion marmalade recipe to use as a rough guide, then promptly forgot all about it.

Then one weekend some months later, some beautiful, massive garlic bulbs in my fridge, the garlic-jam ponder resurfaced. I spent a pleasant evening peeling and slicing forty cloves of garlic, and ended up with two jars of this sweet, punchy, unapologetic condiment. You can serve it on toast with freshly sliced ripe tomatoes, or with buttery sautéed mushrooms, or dolloped on the side of a curry, roast pork or chicken or lamb, or spread it wherever takes your fancy.

MAKES 2 SMALL JARS

350g cloves of garlic
a little oil
70ml light-coloured vinegar
70ml apple juice or white wine
300g sugar
6 thyme stalks, leaves picked, or 1 tsp mixed dried herbs

TIP: *If you find peeling the cloves hard work, chop the top and bottom off and drop them into a jug or bowl of boiling water. Allow to soak for a few minutes – they should slip right out of their skins.*

Peel and slice your garlic cloves and toss into a heavy-bottomed pan with the oil. Bring to a very low heat to soften for 10 minutes – don't allow them to brown or burn.

Pour over the vinegar, apple juice or wine and half the sugar, and bring to the boil. Toss in the thyme leaves and reduce the heat back down to a simmer. Simmer for a further 15 minutes to soften, then mash with a masher to break up into small pieces.

Add the remaining sugar and stir well. Bring to the boil and boil vigorously for 5 minutes, stirring well to stop it sticking to the bottom. Add a splash more wine to loosen if necessary.

Remove from the heat and drop a teaspoon of the jam mixture onto a saucer. If it starts to set around the edges, it's good to go.

Pour the jam carefully into warm sterilized jars (see page 90 for how to sterilize jars) and balance the lids on top as they cool. Once cooled, label and seal the lids, and store the jars in the fridge or in a cool, dry place away from direct sunlight.

Delicious with cheese on toast, tomatoes on toast, various sandwiches, or as a dip for crudités.

TO KEEP: Will keep in the fridge in clean, airtight jars for 6 months – although mine never lasts that long!

TRADITIONAL WHITE SAUCE ⓥ

I must admit I barely make white sauce by this method anymore, preferring the speed and ease of the method on page 247, but I felt inclined to include it before I ride roughshod all over it with my maverick edition, as I'm a firm believer in playing by the rules at least once before you tear them up and throw them over your shoulder.

MAKES AROUND 600ML, OR A GENEROUS-SIZED JAR

1 medium onion
500ml milk
2 bay leaves, fresh
    or dried, or ¼ tsp
    mixed dried herbs
2 cloves (optional)
a pinch of salt
a little black or
    white pepper
50ml light cooking oil
50g flour

First peel your onion, then slice it into quarters and place in a large saucepan. Pour over the milk and add the bay leaves or herbs, cloves, salt and pepper. Warm gently on a medium hob ring to mitigate the risk of it boiling over, then remove from the heat as soon as it starts to bubble. Stand it to one side to cool completely for at least 30 minutes, to allow the flavours to infuse.

When cool and subtly flavourful, strain the milk through a fine-mesh sieve or a colander lined with a couple of sheets of kitchen roll. Keep the onion to use for something else – don't throw it away! Set the infused milk aside for a moment, and rinse out your saucepan to use for the next step – it saves washing up two pans!

Pour the oil into the pan and place on a medium heat for a minute. Add the flour, a third at a time, and whisk continuously to beat it in smoothly. This forms a paste called a roux.

When the flour and oil are combined, add the milk a little at a time, continuing to whisk briskly and steadily until all incorporated and completely smooth. Turn the heat down low and cook for 6–8 minutes, until it thickens. The white sauce will continue to thicken as it cools, so if you are making it in advance, you may wish to add a splash of extra milk or water to keep it loose enough to handle.

TO KEEP: It will keep in the fridge in a clean, lidded jar for 3 days, or in the freezer for 3 months. It may separate when defrosting, just give it a good stir to bring it back together again, and perhaps a pinch more flour if it's a little stubborn.

TIP: *A roux is traditionally made with melted butter, but oil is just fine for the purposes of a basic sauce. If you flip over any jar of remade 'white sauce' in the supermarket, some of the most expensive and upmarket brands are made with oil instead of butter, which is all the justification I need to do it here in a budget cookery book!*

INSTANT CHEESY MASH

It feels more than a little bit cheeky including this as a 'recipe', but it's an instantly gratifying comfort food that I keep a large jar of on standby in my kitchen, and as slovenly as it is, sometimes that's exactly what's required. The cheese you need for this is the dried kind in a tub that's stored on the shelf, not in the fridge, otherwise it won't keep.

MAKES A DECENT-SIZED JAR

360g instant mashed
    potato flakes
180g dried skimmed
    milk powder
50g dried hard
    strong cheese

TIP: *You could crumble a couple of stock cubes into the mixture to give it a gorgeous, comforting flavour.*

Simply place all of the ingredients into a mixing bowl and mix well with a fork to combine. Transfer to a large jar or two, and write the following on it:

'Instant cheesy mash. Add 5ml water per 1g powder.'

To make it, simply follow the above formula. Weigh the required amount of instant cheesy mash powder into a jug, and multiply by 5 to get the volume of water. Add the water, stir well, and microwave for 1 minute. Remove carefully, stir again, and repeat. Depending on how much mash you are making, you may need to increase the timings, I generally allow for 45g of instant cheesy mash powder per person as a side dish, or double that if it's a midnight solo-carb sesh at the end of a terrible day.

TO KEEP: This will keep for 4 months in an airtight, clean jar in a cool, dry place.

INSTANT WHITE SAUCE Ⓥ

I'll take the criticism on the chin for how unorthodox this is, because in the real world, my friends have said this is an absolute game-changer. If it really gives you the willies to even consider it, feel free to use the method on page 244, but having worked in a fair few professional kitchens over the years, you'd be surprised at how many of them use a method very similar to this. And if it's good enough for the real experts, well, it's good enough for me.

MAKES AROUND 600ML, OR A GENEROUS-SIZED JAR

500ml milk
¼ tsp mixed dried herbs
a pinch of salt
a little black or
    white pepper
50ml light cooking oil
50g flour

Measure all of your ingredients into the large cup of a small bullet blender, and blend until smooth. Pour into a jug and microwave for 90 seconds. Remove, stir well, and return it to the microwave for 90 seconds more. Allow to cool and thicken.

TO KEEP: It will keep in the fridge in a clean, lidded jar for 3 days, or in the freezer for 3 months. It may separate when defrosting, just give it a good stir to bring it back together again, and perhaps a pinch more flour if it's a little stubborn.

INSTANT CHEESE SAUCE

In the same style as the instant cheesy mash on page 245, this instant cheese sauce is a handy helpmeet for quick stress-free dinners, and it works out far cheaper than buying the individual packets of the stuff.

MAKES A DECENT-SIZED JAR

4 tbsp plain flour
200g dried skimmed
    milk powder
50g dried hard
    strong cheese
a few pinches of salt
plenty of black pepper

Simply place all of the ingredients in a clean jar with a tight-fitting lid, and shake well to combine.

To make it, spoon 2 tablespoons of the instant cheese sauce mixture into a small saucepan, along with 2 tablespoons of light cooking oil. Mix well on a low heat to combine, then gradually add 200ml of boiling water, stirring well to combine. It will thicken as it warms through, so adjust the water levels to your desired consistency.

TO KEEP: The dried mixture will keep for up to 6 months in a clean, airtight jar, in a cool dry place away from direct sunlight. Shake well to redistribute the contents before using as they may settle. Once made up, the cheese sauce will keep for 3 days in the fridge. Not recommended for freezing.

PEACH CHUTNEY (Ve)

A delicious alternative to mango chutney as an accompaniment to curries, or a fantastic addition to cheese on toast, this sweet and spicy condiment is mere minutes' work. And it makes a sweet gift for friends and family, too.

MAKES 2 MEDIUM JARS

2 tins of peach slices or halves, in syrup or juice

8 fat cloves of garlic

20g fresh root ginger

4 tbsp light cooking oil

250ml light-coloured vinegar

120–220g sugar – use less if the peaches are in syrup, more if they are in juice

1 tbsp cumin, seeds or ground

1 tsp chilli flakes or powder

½ tsp salt

plenty of black pepper

Drain the peaches, reserving the syrup or juice for later. Chop them roughly, and pop them into a large, heavy-bottomed saucepan.

Peel your garlic and slice it thinly, then add it to the pan. Grate or finely chop the ginger and add that too.

Add half of the oil, and the vinegar, sugar, cumin, chilli, salt and pepper, then pour half of the reserved juice or syrup into the pan. Bring to the boil, then reduce to a simmer. Simmer over a medium heat for 20–45 minutes, until thick and glossy.

Remove from the heat and divide between two sterilized jars (see page 90 on how to sterilize jars), leaving an inch of space at the top if freezing. Add 1 tablespoon of oil to the top of each jar to create a barrier between the chutney and the air, then screw the lids on tightly. Label each jar and leave to cool completely.

TO KEEP: Store in the fridge, and use within 6 months if unopened, or within 2 weeks once you've started to dig in!

PICKLED PINK EGGS ⓥ

An ideal way to preserve a quantity of eggs that may be on the way out – turn
them into a delicious high-protein snack that's ideal for any time of day.

MAKES 6

6 eggs
small raw beetroot or
  a fistful of beetroot
  peelings
300ml red wine vinegar
100ml cold water
75g sugar
a few generous
  pinches of salt
½ tsp black pepper
2 bay leaves (optional)

First test your eggs to see if they are still good – you can do this by popping
them into a bowl of cold water. If they don't float they are good to eat.

Bring a pan of water to the boil, keeping a bowl of cold water to one side as
you'll need that in a moment. Carefully add the eggs one at a time, then set a
timer for 10 minutes. Simmer the eggs for 10 minutes to hard-boil them.

While the eggs are simmering, dice or coarsely grate your beetroot or chop
your peelings and add to a separate pan. Add the vinegar, water, sugar,
salt, pepper and bay leaves, if you're using them. Bring this pan to the boil,
then reduce the heat slightly but so it remains at a vigorous simmer. Keep this
simmering while the eggs boil, and stir it occasionally to dissolve the sugar.

When the 10 minutes are up, remove the eggs from the boiling water with
a spoon, and place them straight into the bowl of cold water to stop them
cooking any further and to cool them enough to safely handle. Remove the
pickling liquor from the heat and allow it to cool slightly,

When the eggs are cool enough to touch, crack the outer shell and peel it
away gently. Place each egg carefully into a very clean, large jar. Pour over
the pickling liquor, until the eggs are covered and the jar is full.

Screw the lid on tightly, and leave to cool completely at room temperature,
then transfer to the fridge.

TO KEEP: The eggs will deepen in colour the longer you manage to
resist them, and if stored correctly, they will keep in the fridge for a couple
of months.

INSTANT HUMMUS Ⓥ

Making your own hummus is super simple, and this recipe uses the entire tin of chickpeas, including the juice. I have flavoured this fairly traditionally, but the possibilities for your own interpretations are limitless.

MAKES ABOUT 275G

1 x 400g tin of chickpeas
1 small clove of garlic
2 tbsp light cooking oil
1 tbsp lemon juice
a pinch of salt
plenty of black pepper

Tip the chickpeas, and the liquid from the tin, into a small bullet blender. Peel the garlic clove, and add that along with the oil, lemon juice, salt and pepper.

Blend everything to a chunky paste and taste it to check the seasoning. Add more lemon, salt or pepper as you like it – be aware that the garlic flavour will intensify as it develops – then transfer it to an airtight container.

TO KEEP: Store it in the fridge until needed. It will keep for up to 5 days.

DUSTBIN PICKLES Ⓥ

So-called because this is where the sad bits of veg in my fridge often end up instead of going in the compost bin. This recipe changes depending on what needs using up, and it works well with red or white cabbage, beetroots, carrots, radishes, onions and much more besides.

MAKES 1 SMALL JAR

300g mixed vegetables
200ml light-coloured vinegar
200ml water
1 level tsp salt
4 tbsp any sugar
oil, for sealing the jar

Finely slice or dice your veg so it is all roughly equally sized, then pop it into a large saucepan. Add the vinegar, water, salt and sugar, and bring to the boil. Boil vigorously for a few minutes, then reduce to a simmer. Simmer for around 15 minutes, until the veg is soft and the salt and sugar have dissolved.

Transfer the veg and the pickling liquor to a clean, sterilized jar (see page 90 for how to sterilize jars). Push the veg down so it is completely submerged in the liquid. Add a splash of oil to the top of the jar to create an airtight seal, screw the lid on tightly, and label it. Pop it in the fridge for safe keeping.

TO KEEP: It will keep in the fridge undisturbed for up to 3 months, and once opened, simply add a little more oil to the top to replace the airtight layer.

SNACKY BEANS (Ve)

I have made many variations on these beans over the years, and they remain one of my favourite from-the-fridge snacks. Ideal for a simple salad, a side dish for cold meats, warmed through to serve with fish, or just eaten from the jar, the potential for experimentation here is enormous. This particular iteration tastes to me like summer by the spoonful, and I hope you enjoy them as much as I do.

MAKES 1 VERY LARGE JAR, OR 2 DECENT-SIZED ONES

2 medium onions

1 whole head of garlic

2 x 400g tins of borlotti, cannellini or butter beans

12 cherry or baby plum tomatoes

1 fresh pepper, any colour, or 150g frozen sliced peppers

350ml light-coloured vinegar

175ml cold water

2 tbsp lemon juice

100ml sunflower oil

4 tbsp any sugar

1 tbsp mixed dried herbs

1 tsp salt

plenty of black pepper

Peel and finely slice your onions, then peel the garlic and halve each clove lengthways. Pop these in a large saucepan. Pour over the beans, including some of the liquid from the tin.

Quarter the tomatoes and slice your pepper, then add these too. Pour over the vinegar, water, lemon juice and oil, and add the sugar, herbs, salt and pepper.

Bring the pan to the boil, then reduce to a simmer. Simmer for 20 minutes, stirring to dissolve the salt and sugar and mix everything together.

Allow to cool for a few minutes off the heat, then transfer to your clean, sterilized jar or jars (see page 90 for how to sterilize jars). The oil will rise to the top of the jar to create an airtight seal, which will keep your beans from spoiling. Label the jars, and pop them in the fridge for a week for the flavours to develop. Try to resist a sneaky snack on them in the meantime; your patience here will pay dividends!

TO KEEP: They will keep in the fridge for up to 3 months unopened. Shake well before opening to redistribute the dressing for best results. Once you make a start on a jar, simply top up with a little oil to replace the airtight seal at the top if required.

YOGHURT CHEESE ⓥ

Inspired by the Middle Eastern 'labneh', this is an ideal use for plain yoghurt on the turn, extending its shelf life and turning it into a delicious dip or snack. I have left the flavour deliberately simple to allow you to experiment with what you have in stock – you can add dried herbs, mixed seeds or any combination of flavours and spices that take your fancy.

MAKES ABOUT 500G

½ tsp salt
1 tbsp mixed dried herbs
500g natural yoghurt
4 tbsp light cooking oil
plenty of black pepper

Stir the salt and herbs into the yoghurt to thoroughly combine them.

Line a bowl with a clean, non-fluffy tea towel, clean piece of cotton material or a large muslin square. It needs to be large enough that the edges will drape over the sides of the bowl all the way around.

Pour the yoghurt mixture into the middle of the material. Gather each of the four corners together loosely and tie in a knot, or tie together with clean string or an elastic band.

Insert a wooden spoon or similar beneath the knot, and balance it across a deep pan so the material is suspended and doesn't touch the bottom of the pan. Transfer the whole thing to the fridge for 24 hours to allow the excess liquid to strain away; the weight of the yoghurt and the suspension will do the hard work for you. If you don't have a deep-enough pan, balance a sieve over a bowl and place the cloth parcel into it. Place a small side plate on top and a tin of beans or similar on top of that to weigh it down and force the whey to drain.

When the soft cheese has formed, transfer it to a clean jar or airtight container and stir through the oil, then serve.

TO KEEP: Keep in a clean jar or airtight container in the fridge for up to 1 week.

HOME
SWEET HOME

I could have written an entire book alone for this chapter – perhaps something to bat my eyelashes at my publisher about in the future – but for now here are a few of my favourite everyday home hacks for cutting costs, reusing ordinary bits and pieces, and saving a few things from landfill. I feel compelled to warn you, however, that once you start to look at everything through the lenses of 'how else could I use this?', keeping things for a rainy day can get kind of addictive. I have a whole hoard of nonsense, carefully cleaned and stacked away, waiting for a new lease of life, so if you have hoarding tendencies – and I'm not ashamed to admit that I very much do – tread carefully here! Or get evangelical about your new thrifty wonders with your friends and family, and cheerfully festoon them with carrier bags of kept goodies if you can't use them all yourself. They might even thank you. Maybe. My Mum and I have an informal trade system going whereby she gives me her glass ramekins, and I give her a handful of ringpulls and loo roll tubes in return. I think I have the better end of the deal here, but we're both pretty happy with it.

THINGS TO KEEP
AND REPURPOSE

Fresh Foods
and Store Cupboard

LEMONS, LIMES, ORANGES If you use fresh citrus fruits, keep the squeezed out 'bums' and rinds. Use them fresh with a sprinkle of salt on the exposed fleshy side to clean the grime from around the sink plugs, in the bath and the shower. Pop one in a bowl of water and microwave it for a minute or two to steam off any gunk that's crusted onto the top of the microwave (or anywhere else!). Dry them out and use them as fire lighters for home fires, fire pits, incinerators or BBQs – the oils in the rind make them super flammable and if you're using them in a BBQ they impart a subtly lemony flavour that infuses lightly with whatever you're cooking. Also add them to a jar or spray bottle with water and leave to infuse in the fridge for a couple of days, give it a vigorous shake every now and then, and use this as an all-purpose, all-natural cleaner around the home. Especially good on ceramic surfaces, like the toilet and sink, and for bringing your windows and any mirrors or glass surfaces up nice and shiny.

VINEGAR You can use a 50/50 water and vinegar solution for almost all of your household cleaning – any vinegar will do fine. You can also use the same mixture to get rid of unpleasant smells in the home, like pet odours or lingering smoke or cooking smells. Spray liberally in the offensive area and leave to dry. You can add a few drops of an essential oil if you like, some rosemary stalks, lemon ends or orange peel to add a fragrance, but it's not essential, the vinegar smell is subtle and will fade of its own accord. Vinegar can also help remove limescale and hard buildups from taps.

SALT Useful for cleaning stubborn stains – add a few teaspoons of table salt to a spray bottle or jar, along with a few tablespoons of any kind of vinegar, and warm water. You can add washing up liquid or a fragranced disinfectant if you fancy. Shake well to dissolve the salt in the water, then use to clean hobs, grimy work surfaces, behind the taps, shower heads, etc.

OIL Small quantities are useful for buffing stainless steel, like pots, pans, surfaces, taps etc. Apply with a soft cloth and clean off vigorously in a circular motion. Oil is also good for polishing solid wooden surfaces, like tables, mantlepieces, bannisters etc, to help prevent scratches and also keep dust at bay. Apply a small amount to a soft cloth and work into the wood in a circular or side-to-side movement, adding more as required. Buff away any excess with a clean cloth, and enjoy your smooth clean shiny surfaces.

COFFEE GROUNDS Scatter liberally around the edges of your garden to keep slugs away – they don't like the way that the coarse grounds scratch their sensitive bellies – or decant into a jar and use as an invigorating shower scrub. Because the grounds will already have been warm and wet, they can be a breeding ground for mould if left to their own devices, so if you want to use them in the bath or shower make sure you put them in an airtight jar, stir through a little oil to create a seal against the air, and use within 3–5 days of storing. And always thoroughly chase them down the drain with plenty of water!

Packaging

CEREAL BOXES These can be great storage boxes. Carefully undo the glued seam with either an index finger slipped under the edge, or a small sharp knife. Fold it inside out so the colourful packaging is on the inside, and stick it back together along the seam: PVA glue works, but for durability I prefer to use sellotape. Use to store paperwork, magazines, bills, letters, kids' artwork or anything that could do with being vaguely organized! They tend to be a standard size, so if you have a few of them, they look neat and uniform all lined up together.

FREEZER BAGS Don't throw these away after one use! Turn them inside out, wash them in warm water and washing up liquid, and hang them to dry from a tap, hook, or popped over a mug or similar on the draining board. When completely dry, turn them the right way in again and store for future use.

TAKEAWAY CARTONS With a bit of careful cleaning, both plastic and foil takeaway cartons can be reused many times before consigning them to the recycle bin. To remove

any stains or discolouration, simply soak them in water with a slug of bleach added for an hour or so and they should come up spanglingly clean. Then wash them as usual to remove any residual bleach, dry them, and number the tub and the lid so you know which ones go together before storing them for future use.

READY-MEAL TRAYS Carefully remove any residual plastic that might be sticking to the edges, then clean them thoroughly with a scrubby brush or wire wool to get into the corners. Use foil trays as small roasting dishes, cake or brownie tins, or loaf tins, and plastic ones as drawer or cupboard tidies or for planting seedlings in.

PLASTIC FRUIT/VEG PUNNETS Wash them out and use them as makeshift fridge dividers, drawer tidies, or to plant seedlings in. Most of them already have small holes in the bottom, making them perfect for drainage for cut and come again salad leaves, herbs, and other shallow-rooted plants. Mushroom punnets are usually plenty deep enough to grow small round radishes in!

BREAD BAGS Turn inside out and dust out any loitering crumbs, then turn the right way in again. Store and use them as sandwich bags or wrap, food storage bags, or even for packaging fragile objects.

BUTTER/MARGARINE TUBS Generally the perfect size for storing and freezing portions of leftovers. Give them a good wash and keep a sticky label and a Sharpie on hand so you know what's in them.

SPICE JARS The perfect size for storing 'bits and pieces' – panel pins, paper clips, bits of string, elastic bands, cable ties, screws, odd spare fixings from flat-packed furniture – and they tend to be a uniform size so look very pleasing when you start to accrue a few of them. Soak them in warm soapy water and use a scrubby sponge or wire wool to take the labels and glue off, and then fill them with whatever you fancy.

LOO ROLL TUBES I use these all over the house – individually for keeping paperwork rolled up and tidy, planting out seedlings, keeping small things safely tucked in the corner of a drawer, wrapping awkwardly shaped small presents like a cracker. Then there's the honeycomb method: staple them together top and bottom in a honeycomb formation until you have enough to fill a shelf or a drawer, then use them to store individual cables, glasses and sunglasses, spices, makeup and makeup brushes, stationery, and if you too have a child who just can't seem to roll socks, use them as individual cubbies to keep pairs together neatly without the stress. I spray-painted mine, but honestly, nobody's going to see it but you.

JARS AND THEIR LIDS Glass jars of all sizes are super useful. Use them to store leftovers in. Use them to shake up a drink with ice like you're Tom Cruise in *Cocktail*. Use them to repot small indoor plants, like succulents or herbs. Add some stones or gravel to the bottom to allow for a little drainage so the roots don't get waterlogged. Use them to store fiddly little things. Use them to incentivize yourself or a household member to reach a target, by filling with ring pulls, 1p coins or some other token. Use them to stash little bits of string, ribbon or other bits and pieces. Use them to shake up a salad dressing so it emulsifies in seconds. Use them to make a tea light lantern. Print a favourite photograph and carefully wedge it across the middle, and screw the lid on tight for an instant frame. They make excellent pen

pots, makeup organizers, receptacles for home-made bath salts. Pop some cheap flimsy battery-operated fairy lights in them and use them as a nightlight or bathroom or hallway lantern. Use them to store herbs and spices, tea, pulses and lentils, other ambient goods.

While on the subject of little glass jars, if you treat yourself (or know anyone who does) to those little glass ramekins of puddings, keep the glass ramekins and stack them on top of each other to store spices it the kitchen or odds and ends, like screws, panel pins, paperclips, stamps, loose change – a veritable totem pole of usefulness perches in most corners and on many window ledges of my home. And if you happen to also enjoy a certain 'once you pop you can't stop' brand of snacks-in-a-tube, the lids from those tubes fit perfectly onto the aforementioned glass ramekins, making the stack a little more solid and the whole thing rather pleasing to look at.

TIN CANS Tin cans are Very Useful. In my house alone right now I have at least thirty, all cleaned out and repurposed as pen pots, a place for various nails and screws and fixtures and fittings, one for sunglasses in the hallway, one for makeup brushes, mascara, and eyeliners in the bathroom. There are a couple in the garden acting as tea light holders with holes jabbed into the side to let the light peek out. There are three on my window ledge with herbs growing out of them. One in the hallway as a change pot for shop runs, and another one for house keys, and another for decanting 'pocket junk', and one next to the washing machine for 'more pocket junk' – if you have children, or even unruly adults, in your household, you'll know all too well the death rattle of the spin cycle with a handful of change in a forgotten pocket, or the bobbly mush that was once a tissue or shopping receipt that seems

to multiply and stick to every inch of the clean washing! I've left most of the cans in their natural austere silvery state, but some I've painted to match my decor. In the kitchen cupboard to pop open bags of dried herbs and spices, nuts and snacks into so they don't spill. One in the fridge door with an inch of water in to keep fresh herbs, well, fresh. You get the picture. Oh, and a Spam tin makes for an excellently cheerful, if slightly retro, pen pot that fits neatly into lots of tiny spaces.

RING PULLS I keep all my ring pulls as well, from the cat food cans, ordinary food cans, fizzy drinks, and pop them (unsurprisingly) in a tin can in the kitchen. I've superglued some to the bottom of a shelf to hang glasses on (the eye kind, not the drinking kind). I loop them over clothes hangers to double my wardrobe space and hang whole outfits up – handy for school or work uniforms! I've firmly tied a length of them together with garden twine to make a chain for hanging utensils on in the kitchen. Made an industrial-chic necklace and a set of jangly bracelets. Hung pictures on the wall, by supergluing the smaller end on, and tweaking the larger end so it stands away from the back slightly. Used them as tiny pull-handles on a set of ridiculous fiddly wooden drawers, with string looped through. Stitched one inside the top of my handbag to loop my sunglasses through. And another with a miniature carabina attached for my sodding keys.

BUBBLE WRAP Use bubble wrap to block up draughts in windows or doors by taping it firmly down across any gaps. You'll need to remove it and clean with a one part bleach to three parts water solution every few weeks to stop condensation and potentially black mould from building up, but the air pockets and a tightly taped edge will keep the heat inside your home and the cold on the outside of it. I tried this in a

particularly cold winter in a rented house, where temperatures were dropping to -2 in the daytime. One layer did the trick, but two layers made it ridiculously toasty. I only kept it up for the really cold spell, as I do like to peek into my garden, although admittedly I was a lot more efficient with my work once I'd spoiled the view! I hung a cheap sheer voile over mine to mask the bubble wrap but still let the light in. A thin white bedsheet would do the same job!

CARDBOARD The way that cardboard is constructed, in a corrugated layered fashion, means that it traps air between the zigzags and so is remarkably insulating. Save the thick cardboard boxes from any deliveries or that you come across in the wild, flat pack it, and tape it together to fix underneath beds, rugs, mattresses, to provide an extra layer of warmth wherever you may need it.

ENVELOPES, BILLS, LETTERS, CIRCULARS I keep any and all bits of paper that are blank on one side, or as near as damn it, under a tin can filled with pens in my hallway. I admit that I trim away rough edges with a large pair of scissors to keep it looking neat and tidy, and use them liberally for fridge notes, reminders, shopping lists, rough recipe drafts, anything I need to jot down.

Household Favourites

TOOTHBRUSHES Keep old toothbrushes and soak them in a bleach and water solution for an hour or so to get rid of the ick factor of it having spent a few months marauding around inside a mouth, then use it (dry!) to clean the fiddly bits of a mobile phone like the charging port and speakers, computer keys, grouting, taps, around pan handles, sink plugs, shower heads, trainers, the treads of shoes, the difficult bits of the oven and hob, anywhere that requires a bit of fiddly manoeuvring!

BLEACH Add bog-standard supermarket value thin bleach to your sturdy whites wash – think bedding, towels, flannels, dishcloths, to bring everything up spangling new and bright white again. Always check the labels and fibre content of anything before you add bleach to it; I tend to only do this for sheets, pillowcases, bath mats, cotton shirts and T-shirts, and similar – nothing synthetic, delicate or valuable! But the expensive 'whitening powders' are generally just powdered bleach, packaged as something mystical and ludicrously overpriced, so the bottom-shelf own-brand liquid variety will do the same job with gusto. And for a simple mould remover that works just as well as any branded store-bought variety, mix one part bleach with three parts water in a large jar or spray bottle, screw the lid or nozzle on tightly, and shake well to combine. Apply with a clean cloth or spray bottle to windows, ledges, behind taps, or to grubby grouting, leave to work its magic for half an hour, then wipe clean.

LAUNDRY POWDER Use half of the quantity suggested on the box and your laundry will still come up just as clean, but for half the cost.

FAST WASH Almost everything in my home is washed on a 14-minute 'fast wash' cycle, and it almost all comes up immaculate. Anything particularly grubby just goes in again on the next run; but I've saved a fortune by cutting down the time that my machine runs for. Check out your settings and see what the fastest wash cycle is on your machine, and give it a go. The worst thing that can happen is you'll need to fling it through

again, but you might surprise yourself at just how effective the speedy wash can be.

WASHING-UP LIQUID Decant it into a bottle, one part washing-up liquid to three parts water, and shake well to dilute it. It'll still bring your dishes up nice and clean, but last you four times as long. I learned this from my grandad, who would continue to dilute it as the bottle ran out until it was almost clear and barely sudsy, and yet everything in his kitchen was always immaculate.

WIRE WOOL Your best friend in keeping a spotless armoury of kitchen equipment; a single piece is essential for scouring off burned-on grease or food stains, stubborn unidentifiable murk in the corners of roasting dishes and baking trays, stainless steel pans, and more. Keep it clean and dry when not in use and it will last for months – don't waste money on the 'soap filled pads' that go rusty after a single use, instead get yourself some cheap scrubby wire wool and soap it yourself with a little washing-up liquid for an almost everlasting extra pair of hands in the kitchen.

SOCKS Odd, mismatched, holey or worn? Keep them for buffing windows, cleaning blinds, polishing surfaces, or fill with rice and lavender and twist and fold back on itself to make a microwaveable hot pocket for sore joints or cold nights. Make sure there are no metallic threads or embellishments on them though if you're planning to put them in the microwave: they'll get a lot hotter than you bargain for!

OLD T-SHIRTS Excellent for drying long or thick hair, also cut up and use as general cleaning cloths, for polishing windows and glass, getting taps gleaming, etc.

TUMBLE DRYER FLUFF If you have a tumble dryer, you'll hopefully know you should be cleaning out the fluff catcher after or before every single use, to prevent it catching fire. With my old hat on, I cannot stress strongly enough how many house fires are started in the tumble dryer, and how infuriatingly preventable it is. Get into the habit of cleaning out your fluff filter and popping it all in a jar. Instead of leaving it as a silently ticking bomb in the filter section of the machine, pull it out and harness its remarkable flammability for good. Stuffed into an old toilet roll tube, with the ends slightly squished in to loosely keep it in place, it makes for a terrifyingly effcient firelighter for home fireplaces, garden fire pits, starting off a BBQ (make sure it's all completely burned away before putting any food on it!). Use it to kickstart a garden incinerator, if you're into that kind of thing.

TUMBLE DRYER WATER Condenser tumble dryers usually collect water in the bottom tray, door, or top drawer, depending on which model you have. I rarely use mine, preferring the outdoors or a collection of wobbly airers (or hangers precariously perched from picture rails, for shirts and things) but when I do, I reuse the water to mop the floor with and do other cleaning tasks. Simply decant it into recycled large drinks bottles and store it under the sink until needed. It already smells delicious from the strained-out detergent from the wash, and can be used for general cleaning all over the house.

CHIPPED MUGS Use them as flowerpots for growing herbs, pen pots, storing odd screws or panel pins or elastic bands, in the hallway for keys or sunglasses, as a toothbrush holder, or anything that takes your fancy rather than throwing them out. If you're using them for planting, add some stones or gravel to the bottom to allow for a little drainage so the roots don't get waterlogged, then make yourself a little garden tea party feature by repotting supermarket herb plants or growing some from seeds.

HAND TOWELS It's taken some practice, but both I and my son can dry our entire bodies after a shower with just a hand towel and a bit of vigorous application. (I have actually perfected this down to the humble flannel, but I recognize this may be a step too far for most people!). Using a smaller towel may be a subtle shift, but they take up far less space in the wash than a bath sheet, meaning fewer washes, meaning a little money saved along the way. And all of these incremental changes do add up significantly over time.

FLANNELS I am almost evangelical about facecloths; I keep a stack of them in my bathroom to use morning and evening and any time in between. Forget spending money on fancy face wipes and just go back to basics with a clean flannel and hot water; your skin and your wallet will thank you for it.

NEWSPAPERS AND MAGAZINES I keep newspapers, free circulars, and magazines to use as gift wrap for presents, tied up with string with homemade labels cut from old greetings cards. I've been doing this for so long that my friends and family think it charming and quirky; and I do admit to greatly enjoying trying to find headlines or photographs that will either match or tickle the recipient. Gift wrap is so quickly torn apart and discarded for the treasure within that it feels incredibly frivolous to spend any money on it; and by reusing newspapers and the like, you get to feel a little virtuous about its recyclability, too.

HOME HACKS TO SAVE YOU MONEY

THERMAL FLASKS If you like to drink hot drinks throughout the day, boil the kettle in the morning and decant the hot water into a large thermal flask to use all day instead of re-boiling the kettle multiple times. I've also done a small set of almost-no-energy recipes that use a thermal flask and some patience to cook them in place of a hob. Head over to cookingonabootstrap.com and search for 'thermal flask' to find them.

HOT-WATER BOTTLES Again, instead of heating the entire house to keep warm, try filling a hot-water bottle and placing it across your stomach or strapped to the small of your back. It's surprisingly effective, while being far cheaper than pumping warm air through the whole heating system. And if you have a fever, insanely hot weather, or hot flushes, half fill one with cold water and stand it in the freezer with the lid off, folding the top over and wedging it in to a full drawer to keep it upright, for an hour or two until the water has frozen. Fill to the top with cold water and screw the lid on tight, and use it as a cold water bottle to cool yourself off.

SOLAR LIGHTS I bought cheap solar garden lanterns a couple of years ago and parked them on the window ledges throughout the day; at night they hang in the hallway, one as a nightlight in my son's bedroom, and one perched on the toilet cistern. It saves us from having multiple lights on overnight without feeling like we live in a horror movie, and the soft glow is just enough to guide us to the loo or read a book under the duvet.

ELECTRIC BLANKET I have a small single electric blanket on my sofa, underneath a throw, and one on mine and my son's beds. Instead of heating the entire house in the cold-but-not-unbearably-so parts of the year, I simply heat whatever we happen to be sitting or snoozing on at the time. I can't recommend this highly enough.

CHARITY-SHOP GIFTING There's a real joyous challenge in trawling my local charity shops to find gifts for birthdays and other special occasions. It usually means that I am shopping with the recipient firmly in mind, rather than panic buying some mindless homogenous junk, and can laser focus on what they might be delighted to receive rather than be swept up in trends and societal expectations. Treasures over the years have included a leather-bound hardback set of the complete works of Charles Dickens, some nearly new Christian Dior high-tops, a Vivienne Westwood dress, the missing pieces of a Royal Albert tea set plus some extras for me, a genuine 1970s Marks & Spencer tea tray, a Radley handbag, an awful lot of Wedgwood, a fully working Tracy Island with Thunderbirds 1 through to 5, a Karl Marx pocket watch, two immaculate copies of *Mrs Beeton's Book of Household Management* and a naff solar-powered figurine of the Queen doing a royal wave in the style of those lucky Chinese cat toys. Start early, to give yourself a chance to browse. The triple win of purchasing something that isn't contributing to landfill, donating to a good cause, and saving yourself an absolute fortune, is worth pursuing.

INDEX

Page numbers in **bold** indicate photos.

THANK YOUS

Firstly Rosemary – a person I describe to my friends as 'a cross between a good doctor's receptionist, erstwhile therapist, and the cool auntie you never want to disappoint', but who is actually my long-suffering agent and the person who always picks me back up and pops me on my paws when I want to throw it all in and hide in my duvet. I don't know why you put up with me or how I got so lucky as to still be working with you, but as long as your blood pressure can handle the elasticity of time where my email inbox is concerned, long may we continue. I wouldn't be here without you, and the 'here' is physical, mental, spiritual, as well as in the metaphysical pages of yet another book. My best yet, and I mean it this time. Until the next time, of course. Supporting Rosemary (by which I mean usually emailing me to tell me to read my emails!), the patient and ever-cheerful Matt and Natalia. Thank you for everything and I really am very sorry I am quite so shit at deadlines. Matt, you're new enough to still believe me when I say I'll do better, but try to ignore the stifled laughter from your longstanding colleagues when I say it in earnest.

Carole – lovely Carole, my publisher and dear friend. I grow and nurture these ideas for months on end, and then like a new parent standing at the first-day-of-school gates chewing my fingers I entrust them to your hands, and every time I am absolutely delighted to see them take shape and grow in the Bluebird nursery. It's a testament to your grace and compassion that you have such a strong and glorious team around you, especially the ever-patient and gentle Martha without whom this book would be a rough-hewn shadow of what it is today. And thanks also to Jodie, Sian and Zainab for all their co-starring roles in pulling together all the tedious and often thankless back room logistics that turn my walls of words into a marketable and hopefully mildly useful product.

And to all of my readers, whether you bought this book, were gifted it, borrowed it from the library, or found it in a charity shop, thank you for taking the time to pore through my jumble of words and I hope there is something within that is helpful to you.

And to all of my followers on various social media platforms: thanks for all the doggos, prayers, kind words, and tweets about your favourite sandwiches. Being a self-employed writer is an isolated and often maddeningly lonely business; and having hundreds of thousands of friends in my pocket helps a great deal with keeping the rough edges of that away when it's needed. Each and every one of you make my absolute day when you get in touch to ask a food-related question, show me a random collection of tins in your cupboard and fire up my creative synapses trying to put them together into ideas for dinners, send sympathy when varying bits of my body are misbehaving, and the community that gathers around in the cyberspace whenever there are food banks to stock, funds to raise, advice to give, or just photos of your cats being assholes, is something I'm always bowled over by anew every time.

To the shameless namedropping section, but you'll know the reasons why you're included here and the roles you have played in keeping me on my feet, on the ground, supported and gently advised and just being all-round decent human beings when I needed you the most; my gratitude for having you in my life, in my phone, in my ear, or across many a lunch table in a very dark period is inexpressible even with my tendency to absolute verbosity: Nigella Lawson, Matt Tebbutt, Rhianna Pratchett, Mark Lewis, Jay Rayner, Matthew Freud, Richard Osman, Emma Freud, Russell Brand, Nigel Slater, Eamonn Holmes, Linda Riley, Melanie Rickey, Laurie Penny, Owen Jones, Rupa Huq, Billy Bragg, Gary Lineker, Moose Allain, Ralf Little and many more besides.

To my parents, Evelyn and David, for absolutely everything. Especially over the last couple of tumultuous and unprecedentedly challenging years: for the values you instilled in me as a child and the love and support and patience and telling me to stop being a tit when I'm being a tit. You keep me grounded, but also oil my wings so I can flit about doing all the things I do, and I don't tell you enough how grateful I am for every day I've lived in your genetic mishmash and under your care. Even at 34 years old, whenever I find myself in a pickle, a cup of tea round my parents' house usually sorts it out. (A roast dinner is even better!)

To Kris, and Faith and Peter, and Joy and Nikki, of all the families I could have found myself accidentally in the middle of, I'm so thankful it was yours. Through everything, from the Before Times to the Terrible Times to the Mad Accidentally Famous Times to the Whatever This Bit Holds Next Times, you've helped provide love, security and stability for our very precious boy, and for that I will feel forever blessed. And Brian, I hope you know that that gobby little wretch you took a chance on employing in your coffee shop all those years ago kind of turned out alright in the end.

To Sammy and Lisa, for literally keeping me alive in ways that only you know about over the last year and before then, for nagging me to get this done with love and support and bollockings and exasperation, for always being on the end of the phone or a cup of coffee, and for being absolutely excellent human beings. I'm very very glad to have you both in my life, and for someone who has just written 70,000 words here I can't seem to find the right ones to express my gratitude for you both. Lisa, this is the book that was on my 'things to finish before graduation' list, and, well, this really, REALLY wouldn't exist without you. And neither would I, probably, so, cheers.

To Russell, Chip Somers, Tony OD, Dawn and Nikki, for your presence, guidance, suggestions, and at times, the mildest of absolutely necessary rollockings. For nudging me gently back onto the right track, right-sizing my bonkers thinking, and being the cornerstones of the foundations from which I am rebuilding the wreckage of my life, one day at a time.

To Georgi and Caz, and the best boy Bodie, for endless cups of tea and listening to my monologues because I work from home by myself and have entirely forgotten how to be a social being at the best of times. Awareness is the first step to change, apparently. I'm working on it. I am in the process of closely observing the human species and attempting to imitate their behaviours so that I may one day pass for one of their number – but with you two I can fully be my mad, ADHD, stream of consciousness, utterly batshit self, and I'm not sure what you both did in a previous life to deserve that particular penance, but boy am I glad to have you around. And you know, I do make the odd cake sometimes, so I hope it kind of all balances out.

To Jenny, Peter, Barbara, and everyone else who invariably told me in my formative years that I was 'never going to amount to anything', 'only going to be good for making burgers' and 'not my f**king problem' – you were partly right, I suppose. I only amounted to the grand height of five feet and one point seven inches, being cast out from a secure lifetime job into poverty and destitution turned out to be the defining rock bottom from which I painstakingly and entirely accidentally built whatever this incredible life is now, and as it turned out the career advice was fairly sound after all, because I am in fact incredibly good at making burgers.

And finally, Jonny. Or Jonathon, as he's 12 now and cocks an eyebrow at me when I call him Jonny in front of people. It's still mildly incredible to me that I'm somehow in charge of a small human and have inexplicably managed to keep him alive for almost 13 years. I can't even keep a succulent or a front door key for three months at a time, but you seem thankfully fairly resilient. I'm so proud of you every day – despite the turbulence of my life throughout the whole of yours, you've emerged hilarious, self-assured, emotionally resilient, kind, smart and pretty handy with a drying-up cloth. I love you more every day; more than I ever thought my heart could hold but it just expands to squish more in, and you amaze me constantly in myriad and beautiful ways. Maybe this will be the book that gets us our forever home, where we can paint the front door turquoise and plant hydrangeas in the garden and still be there in the spring to watch them grow. I love you, pickle, and as you are sassily keen to remind me, I'd still be in the Fire Service if you hadn't come along. I did enjoy that, but boy oh boy what an adventure we're having now.

First published 2023 by Bluebird
an imprint of Pan Macmillan
The Smithson, 6 Briset Street, London EC1M 5NR
EU representative: Macmillan Publishers Ireland Ltd, 1st Floor,
The Liffey Trust Centre, 117–126 Sheriff Street Upper,
Dublin 1, D01 YC43

Associated companies throughout the world
www.panmacmillan.com

ISBN 978-1-0350-0851-3

1 3 5 7 9 8 6 4 2

A CIP catalogue record for this book is available from the British Library.
Printed and bound in China.

Publisher Carole Tonkinson
Managing Editor Martha Burley
Assistant Editor Zainab Dawood
Production Manager Sarah Badhan
Design and Illustration Hart Studio
Food and Prop Styling Pip Spence

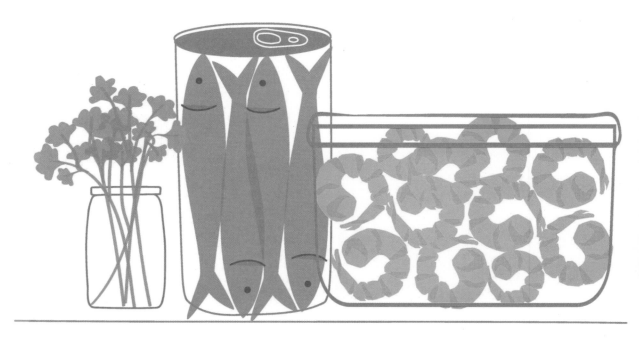